MUSTARD SEED
FAITH

MUSTARD SEED
FAITH

DON'T HYBRIDIZE YOUR FAITH WITH
CONTAMINATED SEEDS FROM THE ENEMY.

BY
HANSIE STEYN

XULON PRESS

Xulon Press
2301 Lucien Way #415
Maitland, FL 32751
407.339.4217
www.xulonpress.com

Printed in the United States of America.

ISBN-13: 978-1-54565-242-8

CONTENTS

Introduction

Faith! What an incredible treasure and power that God has given to mankind. It is a power that every person has and that God wants us to use. "Does every human being have faith?" you may ask. Yes, even unbelievers have been given faith. Romans 12:3 says, "For I say, through the grace given to me, to everyone who is among you, not to think of himself more highly than he ought to think, but to think soberly, as *God has dealt to each one a measure of faith*." Since the day that we were born we had been given faith. That's why a baby trusts his mother. The baby doesn't know that it has to have faith in God. It's been given faith by God and starts exercising that faith immediately by trusting that his mother is going to feed and look after him. We all did that from day one of our lives. Isn't that incredible how God dealt each and every person that was born a measure of faith? We have to take that faith and start using it towards God and having faith in the One who created us, God! So God has given every one of us the measure of faith. Why? So that we could get saved. God made sure that every person had enough faith to believe in Him to become their Savior. That's how you and I got saved, right?

So what is faith? In Hebrews 11:1 faith is explained: "Now faith is the substance of things hoped for, the evidence of things not seen." This means that our faith in God is the solid foundation, the pillars, the confidence, reliance, and our dependence on God. Faith is what supports us and holds us up when we pray and ask God for specific needs that we have. It is knowing, accepting, believing, and expecting that God will supply what we need, even though we can't see it immediately—that's faith. We must also understand that we are people of faith. God has given us the gift of faith, and we have to use it. Ephesians 2:8 says, "For by grace you have been saved through faith, and that not of yourselves; *it is the gift of God*." We all need faith, and we all have to use our faith as believers. God gave us the gift of faith for specific reasons, and it is to our advantage. To begin with, let's look at some advantages of having faith and living by faith.

1. We have to live by faith: "For in it the righteousness of God is revealed from faith to faith; as it is written, *'The just shall live by faith'*" (Romans 1:17). As you can see, as righteous believers, we have to live by faith every day of our lives. We have to apply our faith to everyday situations and live by it. We have to trust God for everything we need. We can't put our faith in anyone else but God. We live by faith in God alone.

2. We have faith so we can please God: Hebrews 11:6 says, "But without faith *it is impossible to please Him,* for he who comes to God must believe that He is, and that He is a rewarder of those who diligently seek Him." When we put our faith in God that He will heal, save, deliver, and supply all our needs, that's when we please God through our faith.

When God sees that we're depending on Him and not on anyone or anything else, that's when He's happy, and pleased with us. What a great way to live by faith.

3. We have faith so that we can resist the devil: 1 Peter 5:8–9 instructs us to "Be sober, be vigilant; because your adversary the devil walks about like a roaring lion, seeking whom he may devour. *Resist him, steadfast in the faith*, knowing that the same sufferings are experienced by your brotherhood in the world." When the devil attacks us, we put our faith in God to help us and to protect us, that's how we use our faith to resist the enemy. When Satan creates problems, we demonstrate our faith, and we retaliate with our faith. We let him know that in spite of the attacks, we're putting our faith in God's power and we believe that He's going to set us free and protect us. That's how we resist Satan with our faith.

4. We have faith so that we can fight the spiritual war: 1 Timothy 6:12 tells us to "*Fight the good fight of faith*, lay hold on eternal life, to which you were also called and have confessed the good confession in the presence of many witnesses." We are not fighting a physical battle; we're fighting a spiritual fight. We use our faith to fight the enemy; there is a faith declaration in God's Word that God's power is greater than the power of the enemy and the power of the problem. We fight with our faith, the good fight of faith. We declare victory through our faith, even though we can't see it yet and we fight the spiritual battle by speaking faith-filled words.

5. We have faith so that we can overcome the world and the things of the world: 1 John 5:4 says, "For

whatever is born of God overcomes the world. *And this is the victory that has overcome the world—our faith.*" While we're fighting with our faith, we'll be able to overcome the world and the things of the world. How do we overcome sickness, addiction, depression, etc. and other problems in the world by using faith? We apply our faith to the situation, speaking faith-filled words, believing that we can get healed, that we can get delivered and that we can overcome anything the world throws at us. Worldly situations can only be overcome by having faith in God, and in His Word. Only He can change the situation. Remember that we are overcomers when we believe that all things are possible through our faith in God.

6. We have faith to protect us: Ephesians 6:16 tells us how: "Above all, taking *the shield of faith with which you will be able to quench all the fiery darts of the wicked one.*" Our faith acts as an invisible shield when the enemy attacks. We pick up the shield of faith and we use it as an invisible shield so that the fiery darts or attacks from the enemy are stopped from hurting us. This shield of faith is formed by hearing the Word of God, and it will protect us. The enemy cannot break through this shield of faith, it's too powerful.

7. We have faith so that we can get saved and healed: "For *by grace you have been saved through faith,* and that not of yourselves; it is the gift of God" (Ephesians 2:8). Acts 3:16 states, "And His name, *through faith in His name, has made this man strong,* whom you see and know. Yes, the faith which comes through Him has given him this per- fect soundness (healing) in the presence of you all."

Our faith is necessary when we're believing God to save, heal, and deliver us. Without faith, it won't happen. While every person has a measure of faith to be able to get saved, to be healed, and to be set free, we have to apply our faith towards these promises in the Word of God. We'll discuss this topic more in later chapters.

8. We have faith so that we can be blessed: Galatians 3:9 informs us: "So then *those who are of faith are blessed with believing Abraham*." How does this work? Well, Abraham was the father of faith, and God highly blessed him because he put all his faith in God not knowing when the promise would come to pass. When we trust no one else but God, He will stay true to His promises and that's how we're blessed the same way that Abraham was blessed. Faith in God produces blessings; that's a fact.

9. We have faith so that impossible situations can become possible: Mark 9:23 tells us that "Jesus said to him, '*If you can believe, all things are possible to him who believes*,'" and Mark 11:22–24 further explains:

> So Jesus answered and said to them, "*Have faith in God*. For assuredly, I say to you, whoever says to this mountain, 'Be removed and be cast into the sea,' and does not doubt in his heart, *but believes that those things he says will be done, he will have whatever he says*. Therefore I say to you, whatever things you ask when you pray, believe that

you receive them, and you will
have them.

Jesus was letting us know that when we function by
faith every single day of our lives, that nothing will
be impossible for us. If we can only believe that He
will do what we've asked Him to do, the impossible
will become possible in our lives.

10. We have faith so that we can receive our promises
from God: Hebrews 6:12 says, "that you do not
become sluggish, *but imitate those who through
faith and patience inherit the promises*." Living
and functioning by faith, patiently, on a daily basis
will produce the promises that God has made. Faith
needs patience, like having a twin brother, they have
to work together to be efficient. Sometimes we have
faith but no patience, so we give up. We have to be
able to wait for God to heal, save, and deliver us,
and by faith, we have to hold on to the promises of
God. Sometimes it takes time for the promises to
manifest. Just patiently wait. God is faithful and His
promises will come to pass.

11. We have faith so we can focus on God's promises,
and not to focus on the problem. Second Corinthians
5:7 encourages us to: "*walk by faith, not by sight*."
This is very important in the life of a Christian.
Satan is the one that always creates the problems.
He'll always show us what the problem is, and what
the effects of the problems are going to be. That's
when we look, and see what Satan's doing, instead
of looking and seeing what Jesus has already done
for us. This produces fear because we're focused
on what we're looking at, and we're not focused on
what the answer is, that's on its way. Nevertheless,

we can't afford to function living by fear or by sight. We have to function by faith and believe. We have to hear what the Word of God says about the situation, then we have to believe the answer that's in the Word and accept it by faith. In addition, we have to speak what the Word of God says. This produces faith. By hearing, believing, and speaking the Word of God, we'll counter act what we're seeing. The Word of God is more powerful than that what we're seeing. So, let's apply the Word of God to rise above what we're seeing. That's how we walk by faith and not by sight. Remember we have to have faith in God, and believe that only He can change our situations.

The above scriptures demonstrate how important faith is in the life of a Christian. We definitely need faith, but we also need our faith to work. We have to use our faith on a daily basis as well, not only when we feel like it. Now I just want to make one thing clear. When we put our trust, confidence, reliance, our faith, in God, we're not putting Him in a box and demanding what we want. All we're doing is calling the promises of God into existence. We're claiming the promises that He has already provided for all of us according to His Word, that's what we're doing. To be able to receive God's promises, He wants us to put all the faith that He has given us in Him—not in money, or in people, not in the government, vehicles, homes, jobs, or anything else. In Mark 11: 22, after Jesus had cursed the fig tree, He explained it to the disciples very clearly. He told them that they should have faith in God, remember? Today the same principle applies. We should also have faith in God and in no one else, so that our faith can work and we can see results. When my wife was sick and almost died from a blockage in her intestines, God supplied us with a wonderful Christian doctor. I had to believe what he was medically telling me and what he was going to do to try and save her life. I trusted the doctors expertise but nevertheless, my faith was not in the doctor. My faith was in God that He would use the doctor's hands and give him wisdom with the surgery. You can read her testimony in chapter 10.

That's why, when I pray for people, I always make sure that they realize that they have to have faith in God and not in me or in any one else praying for them. I'm the believer agreeing with them, for salvation, for healing, deliverance, and for whatever we're praying for, but God is the One that actually saves, heals and delivers them. I cannot take God's place. No one takes God's place! We are believers, with the authority and power coming from God the Holy Spirit. God can use people like us, yes, but God should still get the glory for all the miracles and healings. So we have to put our faith in God and not in people. We put our faith in God that He will use the pastor, the evangelist, and other believers who are praying for us, but we never put our faith in people. The reason why is because you'll curse yourself. Jeremiah 17:5 says: "Thus says the LORD: '*Cursed is the man who trusts in man* And makes flesh his strength, Whose heart departs from the LORD." (emphasis mine). As you can see, I'm emphasizing having faith in God alone!

I remember the most important time in my life that I had to have faith in God, it was the day that I got saved. I remember being in such a desperate state that I called out to God for salvation because people could not help me. That day the gift of faith that God had given me was stirred up by the Holy Spirit and was put into action. I had never seen God or believed in Him. I'd never read the Bible and never believed in it. That day I used the gift of faith, that measure of faith that God had given every person, and by faith, I realized I needed the almighty God to help me and save me from destruction. By faith, I prayed a prayer and accepted His forgiveness without even really knowing how it worked. I just remember asking God that if He was real, to please forgive me and save me. I did not know if He had heard me, I just prayed by faith accepting He was going to forgive me.

I did not hear a voice saying that I was forgiven or not. I just believed, and by faith I accepted it, and received His forgiveness and love and was set free as one of the biggest sinners needing salvation. How did I know that God had forgiven me? I could not see it or feel it and had no proof of it. I only had the measure of faith that He had given me. All I know is that I knew, that I knew, that I was forgiven and that it was going to be okay. I had that peace that all was well with my soul. God had heard my cry and had forgiven and saved me. Only later on when I read the Word I realized how the measure of faith that I had received from God was provided for me so that I could accept Him as Lord and Savior. That, my friend, is how all of us got saved—by having faith in God. Isn't He an awesome God that we serve? Only a living God can do that for people. Thank You Jesus. Now listen, that same kind of faith must be applied for our healing, deliverance, prosperity, protection, and towards all our other needs as well.

Let's see what happens next after we get saved? Well, we have to increase and strengthen our faith in God and spiritually grow and become mature in our Christian walk with Christ. How do we do that? The

Bible tell us in Romans 10:17: "that faith comes by hearing, and hearing the Word of God." So, if we want our faith increased and strengthened, we'll have to get into the Word of God and start reading it, hearing it, and start doing what it says we should be doing. The more we read the Word and hear it, the more we're going to believe it, and our faith is going to become greater and more powerful in God. That's what happens after we get saved. Let me put it this way: it's supposed to happen to all Christians after they get saved. Our faith has got to grow and become strong through the Word of God that we hear, speak and do, continually. The problem is many Christians don't follow this faith-path, and after many years of being saved they still battle in their faith life. They have no clue why their faith is not working like it should be working. Sometimes they think their faith doesn't work at all. In the following chapters I'm going to explain to you why I think our faith is not working like it should be working and why many believers are not seeing the results that their faith should be producing.

CHAPTER 1

The Importance of Faith

When Jesus was on earth, He addressed the issue of faith many times. He spoke to every person that He dealt with, about their faith. He encouraged them according to their faith. He never told people that He had healed them or delivered them. He always said; "Your faith has healed you. According to your faith let it be done. As you have believed let it be done to you," and so forth.

So the thought crossed my mind; what about us? If Jesus told people that they were healed according to their faith, could we also get healed, or be set free, be delivered, be prosperous, and get saved according to our faith? I don't know about you, but I want my faith to work in that way. I want to be healed, I want to be set free from all attacks, trials, and tribulations because of my faith as well. If Jesus was on earth today, I would want Him to say to me, "Hansie, your faith has made you well; because of your faith, you are healed. You have overcome your problem because of your faith." Wouldn't that be great? Wouldn't you want that too?

So the next thought came to mind. Why is it not happening to us, and why aren't we seeing it happen in our churches all over the world? What's the problem? Why is our faith not working like in the days of Jesus? Well, let me put it mildly, most of the times it's not working like back then. Anyway, let's see how it worked in the days while Jesus was on earth. I'm going to give you four examples although there are many more similar occasions and incidents in the Scriptures.

1. Remember the centurion who came to Jesus about his sick servant?

> Now when Jesus had entered Capernaum, a centurion came to Him, pleading with Him, saying, *"Lord, my servant is lying at home paralyzed, dreadfully tormented."* And Jesus said to him, *"I will come and heal him."* The centurion answered and said, *"Lord, I am not worthy that You should come under my roof. But only speak a word, and my servant will be healed. For I also am a man under authority, having soldiers under me. And I say to this one, 'Go,' and he goes; and to another, 'Come,' and he comes; and to my servant, 'Do this,' and he does it."* When Jesus heard it, He marveled, and said to those who followed, *"Assuredly, I say to you, I have not found such great faith, not even in Israel!* And I say to you that many will come from east and west, and sit down with Abraham, Isaac, and Jacob in the

2

kingdom of heaven. But the sons of the kingdom will be cast out into outer darkness. There will be weeping and gnashing of teeth." Then Jesus said to the centurion, "*Go your way; and as you have believed, so let it be done for you.*" And his servant was healed that same hour.

— Matthew 8:5–13, emphasis mine

What a testimony. The centurion asked Jesus to come heal his servant. Jesus said great, let's go. Then the centurion says; "Hang on Jesus, You don't even have to come to my house, *just speak the Word* and my servant would be healed." That was enormous faith working right there my friend. That kind of faith got Jesus' attention. He immediately told the people around him that this was "*great faith* and He had not found such great faith not even among the Jews, God's chosen people." Before I move on I want you to make a mental note of the words "*great faith*." We'll be mentioning this phrase again and explaining it in more detail. Okay, so the centurion had great faith, and it worked. Jesus told him afterward to go his way, and as he had believed, it would be done for him. Guess what? That same hour his servant was healed. We need this great faith, my friends. This is the kind of faith that I want. How about you?

2. Next example. Remember the woman with the issue of blood? She had a blood problem, menstruating every day for twelve years. I can only imagine what that was like; certainly it was a lot of torture for twelve years. Look what happened:

And suddenly, a woman who had a flow of blood for twelve years came from behind and touched the hem of His garment. For *she said to herself, "If only I may touch His garment, I shall be made well*." But Jesus turned around, and when He saw her He said, "Be of good cheer, daughter; *your faith has made you well*." And the woman was made well from that hour.

— Matthew 9:20–22, emphasis mine

Once again, this lady had faith that made Jesus stop and turn around because power had gone out of Him. It got His attention. The same scripture in the book of Mark says that He felt the power, (in the Greek, *dunamis*), dynamite power, going out of Him when she touched Him. You see her touch was a touch of faith. Why? My dear friends get this truth today. She had made up her mind before she even got to where Jesus was that she was going to be healed. She was so sure of it that she said to herself; "*If only I may touch His garment, I shall be made well*." You see she didn't wait for a pastor or an evangelist to tell her she was healed. Oh no, she told herself that she was going to be made well. I think we're missing this point. I hear people speaking to themselves and to other people all the time that they're sick, instead of saying that they're healed; they claim their sickness as *my* cancer and *my* diabetes. They should be saying to themselves that they are healed. This woman was not healed when she had said it to herself, but she believed she was going to be healed because she had faith that she would be healed, without seeing or feeling it. She was calling those things that were not as if though they were (Romans 4:17). She was not saying that she was not sick, or denying her sickness. No, she was saying to herself that she was going to be healed. See the difference? That's faith. That's when Jesus stopped, turned around and did not say; "Wow, I'm the Son of God, I'm Jesus, and I just healed you woman." No, Jesus took no credit for the healing but told her that her own faith had healed her. Where did she get faith from. She had a measure of faith given to her by God, but she also built up her faith by hearing herself say that she was going to be healed. She heard those faith-filled words spoken to herself, by herself all the time. That's the kind of faith that works, and that's the kind of faith that we all need; that's a fact. Now remember, the faith that she had was faith in God, not in the people that were with Jesus, or in the doctors that she had visited all those twelve years. Let's look at the next example.

3. Remember the two blind men? These two guys were blind and wanted to see, so someone must have led them as they followed Jesus to where they could talk to Him.

> When Jesus departed from there, *two blind men followed Him*, crying out and saying, "Son of David, have mercy on us!" And when He had come into the house, the blind men came to Him. And Jesus said to them, "*Do you believe that I am able to do this*?" They said to Him, "*Yes, Lord.*" Then He touched their eyes, saying, "*According to your faith let it*

5

> *be to you*." And their eyes were opened.
> And Jesus sternly warned them, saying,
> "See *that* no one knows *it*." But when
> they had departed, they spread the news
> about Him in all that country.

—Matthew 9:27–31, emphasis mine

Once again, Jesus did not take credit for this healing. He asked them if they believed that He could heal them, testing their faith. They answered Jesus and told Him that they believed that they could get healed. That's when Jesus touched their eyes and said, "*According to your faith, let it be to you*." In other words, as you have believed, depending on how strong your faith is, let it be done to you. Well, obviously their faith was strong and powerful enough, and it worked because they were healed; immediately they could see. Do we have this kind of faith? Don't be worried; I'm going to explain how this kind of faith works and how we can function and live by it as well.

4. Remember the Canaanite woman with the demon-possessed daughter? Now this woman was a Gentile, a Greek woman. She had no covenant right to ask Jesus for any privileges or healings or deliverances or anything else. Nevertheless, she threw herself on the floor at Jesus' feet and worshipped Him, asking Him to deliver her demon-possessed daughter. This woman needed mercy and favor.

> And behold, a woman of Canaan came
> from that region and cried out to Him,
> saying, "Have mercy on me, O Lord,

Son of David! *My daughter is severely demon-possessed.*" But He answered her not a word. And His disciples came and urged Him, saying, "Send her away, for she cries out after us." But He answered and said, "*I was not sent except to the lost sheep of the house of Israel.*" Then she came and worshiped Him, saying, "Lord, help me!" But He answered and said, "*It is not good to take the children's bread and throw it to the little dogs.*" *And she said, "Yes, Lord, yet even the little dogs eat the crumbs which fall from their masters' table.*" Then Jesus answered and said to her, "*O woman, great is your faith! Let it be to you as you desire.*" And her daughter was healed from that very hour.

—Matthew 15:22–28, emphasis mine

Jesus did not answer her immediately, until the disciples asked Him to send her away. She was not supposed to even ask Him anything as a Gentile, remember. Then Jesus spoke to her and told her that He was only sent to the lost sheep of the house of Israel. Why did He say that? Well, God's plan was to offer salvation, including healing and deliverance, to the Jews first before going to the Gentiles. Matthew 10:6 confirms this:

These twelve Jesus sent out and commanded them, saying: "*Do not go into the way of the Gentiles*, and do not enter a city of the Samaritans. But go *rather*

7

to the lost sheep of the house of Israel.
And as you go, preach, saying, 'The
kingdom of heaven is at hand.' *Heal
the sick, cleanse the lepers, raise the
dead, cast out demons. Freely you have
received, freely give.*

For I am not ashamed of the gospel of
Christ, for it is the power of God to salvation for everyone who believes, *for
the Jew first and also for the Greek.*

—Romans 1:16, emphasis mine
in both scriptures.

As you can see, God had planned the same blessings
for the Gentiles and for the Greeks, but the Gentiles
were only to receive their blessings later on. Then
the bread story comes up, and Jesus talks about the
bread and the crumbs. What was that all about? Well,
Jews were children of the kingdom. The bread refers
to the benefits that the Messiah was to bring to the
Jews, which included salvation for the body, soul, and
spirit—from sin, sickness, demons, and satanic powers.
These were family rights, legal rights, promised rights,
human rights, divine rights, and redemptive rights for
all the children of God, but, at that time, for the Jews
only. Children could have whole loaves but the dogs
could only have the crumbs. Now the Gentiles were
called dogs by the Jews. Jesus was not being rude but
was merely using the common speech of His people.
Dogs were not cared for in those days. The term was
not offensive. It merely expressed the fact that Gentiles

were outside the covenant rights of Israel. That's why she said; "*Yes Lord: yet the dogs eat of the crumbs which fall from their masters' table.*" The woman acknowledged her position as undeserving and without legal covenant rights to the children's bread. Yet, she used the Lord's own words concerning dogs as grounds for further claim for the deliverance of her daughter.

She told Jesus that even dogs have rights to the crumbs that the master throws away. She knew that the dogs were allowed to receive the crumbs, and it could be given to them. Children have enough bread to spare, so she claimed the scraps for her daughter and won her case. She demonstrated faith like very few people could. This got the attention of Jesus, and again He said: "*O woman, great is your faith! Let it be to you as you desire.*" Jesus could not turn down such faith based upon such a claim. See, even non-believers could use the measure of faith given to them if they can only believe.

It's actually incredible how this Gentile woman humbled herself and was happy with the crumbs, if only she could get her daughter set free and delivered. That was faith, my friend. Are you and I as desperate enough as she was for a miracle? Through the above situation we see that even Gentiles, unbelievers, have faith given to them, and if used correctly, their faith will work for salvation, healing, deliverance, and anything else that they need. If that's the case, then we, as children of God, could and should also be functioning in the same kind of faith and should be receiving the same kind of success as the above examples have shown us. Why? Well, we're children of God, we're supposed to be having the same kind of success in our faith life. It's promised to us in God's Word.

9

Once again, in all of the above examples, Jesus never took the credit for the healings and deliverances. He recognized that all these people had put their faith in God, and according their faith, He released the power for them to be healed and to be delivered. Now this is the problem and concerns that I experience among Christians in our churches. They are not experiencing the working of this kind of faith, and miracles are scarcely happening in the churches anymore. Salvations are at a minimum and deliverances hardly take place anywhere. Yes we have healings, salvations, and deliverances, but not like we should be seeing. Most believers don't even believe in the demonic and spiritual realm anymore. Many believers know this, and they have questions and concerns about it. Believers want more of God and want their faith to work just like the faith of believers worked in the days when Jesus was on earth. Somewhere we have to look into these concerns right? So let's address this.

CHAPTER 2

Excuses Why Faith Doesn't Work

A s I travel all over the country, I realize that many believers have the same problem and the same concerns about faith. I encounter many Christians, born-again children of God, battling with the same faith issues in every church that I minister in. People believe that God can heal him, save, and deliver them, but when it doesn't happen immediately, the first thing that happens, is they question their faith. They don't understand why their faith is not working like it should be working. Some don't believe their faith is working at all. Listening to a lot of believers asking me questions, I realized that there were three main questions asked about faith. Almost ninety-nine percent of the people asked the same questions. Let's look at these questions and try and solve these problems. Let's address this question; "why do believers believe that their faith is not working like it should be working?"

I've come to the conclusion that Satan, the enemy, has been lying to a lot of Christians about their faith. He keeps on telling them that their faith is not working and that it will never work. Satan wants the believer to make excuses why their faith doesn't work, cannot work, and won't work. The first question I always hear and that's been asked many times is this: "Brother Hansie, I don't think I have faith. I definitely don't have faith for healing that's for sure. I know God can heal, but I don't have the faith that my diabetes can be healed. I've been prayed for so many times, and I've trusted God for so long. I've had faith for that God would heal me, yes, but it's not working, I'm not getting healed, so I most probably don't have faith for healing at all. I don't even believe I have faith anymore. At this point of time I'm battling to have faith for any situation attacking me. Why don't I have faith?" This kind of confession and concern coming from born again Christians shocked me. So my question is this; "Have you ever felt this way?" Are you someone who has ever spoken this way and asked the same question? Have you ever thought this way? Well, what a lie from the devil. People are led to believe and think that they don't have faith, although they do believe that God can do all things. That's like exercising a double-minded faith. Let me nullify this lie for you according to scripture:

> For I say, through the grace given to me, to everyone who is among you, not to think *of himself* more highly than he ought to think, but to think soberly, *as God has dealt to each one a measure of faith.*

> —Romans 12:3, emphasis mine

We've used this scripture already, but let's use it again. It plainly tells us that God has given every one of us a measure of faith. So all of us have a measure of faith—for salvation, for healing, for deliverance, for prosperity, for success, and for all God's promises. Don't let the devil tell you that you don't have faith at all for any of the above or for any other need that you have. Just because you cannot see it happening immediately, it doesn't mean that you don't have faith! You tell that liar to get behind you in Jesus name. You start believing that you have a measure of faith, and that it's been given to you by God. The Bible says we all have a measure of faith, so that excuse and lie from the devil is destroyed, immediately. It's not true. We have to get this lie out of our minds, quickly. We have a measure of faith. We have faith, we have to believe it, and use it.

The second question people ask is this: "Okay brother Hansie, I accept that I have a measure of faith that's been given to me. So I do have faith. But I don't think I have enough faith. I think I need more faith, especially for healing, especially for sicknesses like cancer and diabetes, and definitely for salvation for my family members. Why don't I have a lot of faith like other people do?" Oh okay, so some situations need a lot of faith, and others situations need a little bit of faith to be resolved? Have you ever had these thoughts about your faith life? This is another lie from the enemy. It's not true at all. So let's nullify this lie as well:

> And the apostles said to the Lord, "*Increase our faith.*" So the Lord said, "*If you have faith as a mustard seed, you can say to this mulberry tree, 'Be pulled*

13

up by the roots and be planted in the sea,' and it would obey you."

—Luke 17:5, 6, emphasis mine

The apostles asked Jesus to increase their faith. They wanted more faith. There is nothing wrong with wanting more faith and asking for more faith. Nevertheless, what does Jesus say? He doesn't answer them concerning giving them more faith. He tells them to use the faith that they already have by speaking to the situation. Then Jesus tells them to use their faith like a mustard seed. That's when the mulberry tree would be pulled up by the roots and be removed, and be planted in the sea (Luke 17:6).

Jesus keeps on speaking to them and tells them that the tree will listen to them, and will even obey them. What Jesus was trying to let them know and understand, was that they didn't need a lot of faith for a miracle. They only needed faith the size of a mustard seed for the tree to be uprooted. The same principle applies to our faith life today. We only need faith the size of a mustard seed. We all most probably know how small a mustard seed is, right? It's one of the smallest seeds around. Basically it boils down to the point that we don't need faith the size of a mountain to remove a mountain, or faith the size of a mulberry tree to pluck it up by its roots. No, we only need a little bit of faith, the size of a mustard seed, to remove the mountains and the mulberry trees, which obviously represents sicknesses, salvation, attacks, addictions, and all other obstacles and problems in our lives. These problems will listen to us and can be removed from our lives with faith the size of a mustard seed.

So, don't let the devil tell you your faith is not enough. No, you tell him in Jesus Name that you don't need a lot of faith to resist him and to destroy his satanic attacks. You only need faith the size of a mustard seed; that's good enough for God. The reason why the devil's telling us that our faith is not enough, is because he knows that our faith in God is powerful and will produce results and miracles. In spite of that, he still wants us to believe that we can't do anything about the attacks launched against us because we don't have enough faith to do so. So we stay sick, addicted, bound up, living a miserable tortured life as believers believing this lie. Mustard seed faith is enough faith my friends. We only have to use a small amount of faith, the size of the mustard seed, to be able to see God perform miracles in our lives. We'll talk about this in detail a bit later on.

The third question I'm asked is this: "Okay, I know I have a measure of faith. I accept that I don't need a lot of faith, and that I only need faith the size of a mustard seed. The problem that I'm having is this; "I don't think my faith is working like it should be working. It's not functioning like it should, and I'm not seeing results. I've been believing and having faith that God will hear and answer my prayers. I believe that He can heal my body, but it's not working, it's not happening. Why is my faith not working like it should be working brother Hansie?" Many people are speaking in a negative way and saying things like: "We believe God can supply our needs, fix our finances, give us a job, save our spouses and children, deliver us from addictions, and heal us, but it's not happening. All we're doing is just waiting and waiting, I don't think my faith is working." Can you hear the discouragement in these statements? It sounds like people are giving up! Now

15

this question did get my attention because there was a time in my personal life that I had the same problem and the same questions about my own faith not working like it should be working. I realized that this was a big concern for many believers.

Let's be honest, we all want to be healed and have our family members saved. We trust God and believe that He's going to do what we've asked Him, and we believe it's going to happen. We believe that our faith is elevated and strong, we pray and believe that God's working and answering our prayers. But after a few weeks or a few months, after nothing has changed or happened to our situations, that's when we start getting discouraged and we start saying: "Oh my goodness, my faith is not working. Something must be wrong. Why is nothing happening? Why is God not doing something? Where is God? What's wrong? Why is my faith not working. Is God ever going to heal me?" I'm sure most of us have gone down that bumpy road before!

So I asked God to help me understand this question, and understand the concerns that we have about our faith life. Specifically why it's not working correctly? The immediate response I got from God was this: "That's correct Hansie. You are one hundred percent right." God let me know that this question was a legitimate question and a legitimate concern. He told me that this was the problem that we as believers were having when dealing with our faith; our faith was not working like it should be working. It was not that we did not have faith. It was not that we did not have enough faith. No, the problem was that we we're not using and applying our faith correctly. We're not using our faith like it should be used. There is a missing link somewhere. This came as a shocker, and I needed an explanation from God. Isn't God just awesome? He always helps us and gives us knowledge, wisdom, and discernment. He always teaches us what He wants us to know through His Word. Well, God answered my request through His Word and explained it to me like this. I hope you all get hold of this truth.

At this point of time I'd like to give you the explanations and answers to the questions that we have concerning our faith. I believe that the answers would set your faith in motion so that it could start working like it should be working. I want Jesus to say to me: "Hansie, your faith has made you well, it's healed you. Your faith has delivered you. Your faith is great and strong and powerful. Because of your faith you are healed, set free, and prosperous. According to your faith let it be done to you." Wouldn't you like to hear those words spoken to you? I would love to hear Jesus speak those words to me. Let's see why our faith is not working like it's supposed to be working.

CHAPTER 3

What Is Hybridized Faith?

W hat is hybridized faith? I'm sure many of you are familiar with the word *hybrid*, or *hybridize*. I believe. If not, let me quickly explain. The word hybrid is mostly commonly used with vehicles that are sold as hybrid vehicles. Toyotas, Hondas, and other makes are some of them. This means that the vehicle is being powered by two sources of power: gas and electricity. In other words the vehicle is powered by using gas only, or a battery, that is recharged electrically, or a combination of the two, gas and battery. When these vehicles run on gas, or only with electricity, or combined it saves you a bunch of money because your gas mileage is much lower and thus much cheaper. Another example is a wind hybrid system that generates electricity. We see those massive windmills all over the country, and they use the wind power to generate electricity for certain areas and towns. We may also see solar panels that capture energy from the sun's rays as another hybrid system. So these hybrid systems are all powered by two sources, wind and solar panels to produce electricity. The word hybrid also means to crossbreed, or to interbreed animals, plants, cultures, languages and many other species with each other. They are developed when one takes the seeds of two different species or plants and crossbreed them. That's how a new hybridized specie or plant is created. I'm going to use and apply this hybridizing system example to our faith life, so that we can figure out why our faith is not working like it should be working, so here we go.

Let's hybridize animals, and let's hybridize dogs. Let's say you have a German shepherd, and a Great Dane. These two breeds are powerful dog breeds. They are such pure breeds that when you purchase their puppies, you pay a lot of money for them. They compete on dog shows with these pure thoroughbred dogs and compete in dog competitions where they can win prizes and trophies. These dogs have original registered paperwork to show their purity and status as a thoroughbred and purebred specie. Needless to say, they are worth a lot of money because of their pureness and breed. The problem is that as soon as you hybridize or interbreed them with another breed, you crossbreed them, you interbreed their seed, and a new hybridized specie is born. Now that you've hybridized the two dog species, guess what? All of a sudden you have a problem because their hybridized puppies have lost their thoroughbred, pure status. What are their puppies called? What breed are their puppies? They're not a German shepherd or a Great Dane anymore. Maybe a "Great Shepherd." Okay, go ahead and laugh; it's okay. We don't have a name for them because they are now interbred, hybridized dogs. Some call them mongrels. In America, we call them mutts. In Africa we just call them street dogs. These two combined species, are not as expensive as the pure thoroughbreds are. You can't show with them, and you can't compete on dog shows with these hybridized dogs, because they're not thoroughbreds anymore. They're hybridized dogs, and not worth much. Oh they look beautiful and they're great dogs to have as pets. They're good watchdogs and your children can play with them, but they're mongrels, mutts, street dogs, whatever you want to call them, because they've lost their power and purity status through the hybridizing process. You getting this?

Okay, let's take another example. Let's say we crossbreed, interbreed or hybridize fruits and plants. Many people have tried it, and it works. People take different seeds from plants, hybridize them, and some funny-looking fruit or plant develops. Let's take an apple seed and interbreed or hybridize it with an orange seed. It does work, that's a fact. Whatever product is produced from the two seeds that are hybridized will be a mixture between an apple and an orange, right? Let's call it an "orple." You're welcome; go ahead and laugh again. I'm trying to name these hybrids, and it's not easy! This "orple" will, or can look like an apple, and taste like an orange, or the other way round, whichever way. The fact is that it's not a pure apple or pure orange anymore. The two seeds are hybridized, mixed, and they've lost their original purity and maybe their original taste. I actually saw someone the other day hybridize a banana and a kiwi fruit. It was incredible to see the outcome. The new fruit actually looked exactly like a banana with the yellow skin and the form of the banana. When cut open, the inside was the green of the kiwi fruit. It was amazing to see how this crossbred fruit looked, what it tasted like, and how it was formed.

Likewise you can also hybridize many other plants, fruits, and species. It has been done many times.

Nevertheless, always remember that when they're hybridized, they've lost their originality, their taste, power, and purity. Now the next fact is very interesting. If you take that orple seed and replant it again to reproduce an orple, you're wasting your time; it will not reproduce as an apple or as an orange, or as an orple. It's a hybrid fruit, and all hybrids have no life within themselves and cannot reproduce their own kind. The only thing it can produce within itself is death. A hybrid specie cannot reproduce itself, period. It's the same with a mule, which is a hybrid, or crossbreed, between a donkey and a horse. If you take a female mule and a male mule and try and have baby mules, they will not produce a baby mule. The mules are usually sterile because of the genetic differences between horses and donkeys. They are hybridized animals and have no life within themselves and therefore cannot reproduce. Hybrid dogs can reproduce dogs, mutts, street dogs, but they can't reproduce the pure Great Dane or German shepherd again. Interesting!

That's when God spoke to me, and told me that this was exactly what we were doing with our faith life. We were hybridizing, crossbreeding, and interbreeding our faith with other seeds. Our faith was not pure powerful faith like it should be. Our faith had lost its power and it's purity and had turned into hybrid faith—mongrel faith, mutt faith, all because we had hybridized it with other seeds. What other seeds was God talking about?

Then came the final lesson from God. He showed me that we were busy hybridizing, crossbreeding, and interbreeding our faith with seeds of fear, doubt, unbelief, anger, unforgiveness, bitterness, discouragement and many other seeds that the devil was busy bringing our way. God showed me that these seeds coming from the enemy were contaminated seeds. They were sent by the devil to cancel and weaken the power and purity of our faith. Then God showed me that hybridized faith, or crossbred faith, would not work and could not work or produce any results; just like hybridized plants, animals, and fruit could not work and reproduce any results. There is no life or reproduction in hybridized faith. The aim of hybridizing is to infiltrate and weaken our faith. In the end hybridized faith is going to produce death and failure. This was a scary revelation to me.

Well, knowing me, you all know that I wanted scripture to back it up. "Show me and give me scripture for this, Lord," I asked. So why do all these other seeds contaminate our faith and nullify its strength and power? God explained it to me like this: yes, we have faith for certain issues in our life, and we believe that God can take care of all of our problems. We pray to Him, and we ask Him to help us through all the trials and attacks. Then we thank Him for the miracles in advance. Nevertheless, after a month or two when nothing has happened, we start wondering why God hasn't done anything yet. We start questioning why our faith is not working. We wonder if God has even heard our prayers. Where is God? We start doubting. Is God ever going to do something about our situation? Then we start fearing and accepting that most probably He's not going to hear our prayers, or heal us, or even do anything about our problem. It's over; it's finished, that's how we start thinking and speaking. That's when our faith starts to crumble and we feel defeated. We start doubting. We accept that our faith is not working and it's never going to work. Why? The answer is plain and simple; we start hybridizing our faith with the seeds of fear, doubt, unbelief, discouragement and so on, and we don't even realize it. We think our faith is okay, and working, but it's not, it's contaminated. It's hybridized. What a sly deceiving move from the devil. Sometimes we even hybridize our faith with anger, resentment, and hatred toward people and even towards God. We also hybridize our faith with a lot of other contaminated seeds sent by Satan and we don't even realize it. Let me quickly give you an example. Some lady might be wondering why God has healed and saved Susan's husband, but why hasn't He healed her husband. So she becomes angry at God. She becomes resentful and hateful towards Susan. She blames God because He hasn't saved her husband but saved Susan's husband. Oh my, at that moment she's just hybridized her faith with anger towards God and the power of her faith has just been weakened and basically nullified. After a while Susan gets to a point that she can't believe that God is going to save her husband and she accepts defeat in that area. She stops praying and stops believing altogether and stays tormented for a long time by anger and unbelief. Have you ever been there? When we act the same way that Susan did in the above hybridizing example, our faith will also be changed into mongrel faith, or hybridized mutt faith. We'll have faith that looks good, and we'll be using it, believing that it's working, but it's not and never will. We'll keep trusting and believing God for the miracles, but we'll never see it manifest. We'll never receive our victories. Why? Well, it's not thoroughbred pure faith anymore. It's been contaminated, mixed, crossbred and hybridized with the devil's contaminated seeds of fear, doubt, unbelief, unforgiveness, anger, hatred, and so forth. That's how hybridized faith is formed. "So you're telling us that our faith won't work like it should if we hybridize it with fear, doubt, unbelief or any other contaminated seed sent by Satan Hansie," you may ask? "Yes, definitely, and I've

23

got scripture to prove to you that hybridized faith does not work. Let me explain it to you as God explained it to me."

So let's look at scripture and see what God is showing us? How does the contaminated seeds from the enemy interbreed with our faith and become hybridized faith that doesn't work? Let's look at some examples of what hybridized faith looks like and sounds like. Let's use the contaminated seed of unbelief. We have a father asking Jesus to heal his epileptic son.

> "Lord, have mercy on my son, for he is an epileptic and suffers severely; for he often falls into the fire and often into the water. So I brought him to Your disciples, *but they could not cure him*." Then Jesus answered and said, "O faithless and perverse generation, how long shall I be with you? How long shall I bear with you? Bring him here to Me." And *Jesus rebuked the demon*, and it came out of him; and the child was cured from that very hour. Then the disciples came to Jesus privately and said, "*Why could we not cast it out*?" So Jesus said to them, "*Because of your unbelief*; for assuredly, I say to you, if you have faith as a mustard seed, you will say to this mountain, 'Move from here to there,' and it will move; and nothing will be impossible for you. However, this kind does not go out except by prayer and fasting."

> —Matthew 17:15–21, emphasis mine

This man brought his epileptic son to Jesus to be healed because the disciples couldn't heal him. Why couldn't they heal the epileptic boy? Did they not have faith, power and authority to do it? Of course they did. They had all the power and authority that they needed. As a matter of fact, Jesus had previously given all His disciples His authority to go heal the sick, cleanse the lepers, raise the dead, and drive out demons. Why did Jesus give them His power and authority? Well remember, they had not yet received the Holy Spirit and were not baptized in the Holy Spirit yet. So they had not yet received any power from the Holy Spirit. Jesus had to give them His authority, His power, and His Name and He could, because He had already been baptized with Holy Spirit. He received power and authority from the Holy Spirit when John the Baptist baptized Him. So, after giving the disciples His authority, they went around praying for people, healing the sick, and delivering them in every city and all the surrounding areas where they went. They even told Jesus with great joy in Luke 10:17; "that all the demons were in submission to them in His Name." They were so excited that they could heal the sick, drive out demons from many who were possessed, and even raise the dead. This they did with great joy like I said. How were they doing these miracles? They were using the authority that Jesus had given them and using His Name. That's how all these signs and wonders were taking place. So why couldn't they heal an epileptic boy? That's a good question right? When they asked Jesus privately what they had done wrong He answered them. "*Because of your unbelief.*" Or like other translations say: "*Because of your little faith.*" Unbelief is the same as having little faith; remember this. We're going to explain "little faith" later

25

on. Well, they obviously had faith which worked when they did all those other miracles, but for some or other reason, they crossbred, mixed, and hybridized their faith with unbelief when they prayed for the epileptic boy. Why did they do that? Who knows why; the Bible doesn't tell us why. Why do you and I hybridize our faith with unbelief? Who knows why; only we know, right? So their hybridized faith, or little faith, could not heal the young epileptic boy. Newsflash: the contaminated seed of unbelief that is hybridized with our faith, nullifies the power of our pure powerful faith, and our faith doesn't work like it should be working. The young boy could not be healed because of unbelief that was hybridized with their faith, period! So here's the first example that hybridized faith doesn't work. Let's look at another example of what hybridized faith looks like: the seed of doubt. How does doubt stop your faith from working correctly? Remember Peter?

> So He said, "*Come*." And when Peter had come down out of the boat, he walked on the water to go to Jesus. But *when he saw that the wind was boisterous, he was afraid; and beginning to sink* he cried out, saying, "*Lord, save me*!" And immediately Jesus stretched out His hand and caught him, and said to him, "*O you of little faith, why did you doubt?*"
>
> —Matthew 14:31, emphasis mine

What had just happened? Well, the disciples were in the middle of the sea, and a storm came up. It was

26

a bad storm, with strong blowing winds, creating massive waves in the sea. The disciples were worrying and fearing. Jesus came walking toward them on the sea, and when He realized that they were afraid, He calmed them down by saying, "Be of good cheer; it is me, Jesus. Do not be afraid." Now perhaps Peter was not sure if it was Jesus, or perhaps he was just being impulsive Peter again. He wanted Jesus to call him out onto the water and Jesus did just that, and guess what? Peter stepped out of the boat and started walking on the water—something that no other human being had ever done before, except Jesus. What mighty faith Peter was demonstrating. He did not question Jesus when He said, "Come." Just one word from Jesus and Peter had the faith to walk on the water toward Jesus. How did he achieve this miracle? By faith, of course. Where did he get this faith from? From hearing *one word* from Jesus: "Come"; that's it. That one word from Jesus gave Peter the faith to walk on water. Not a whole chapter or twenty verses from the Bible. No, one Word from Jesus gave Peter the faith that he needed. Let's move on. While Peter was walking on the water, all the other disciples were seeing the miracle taking place. All of a sudden, calamity struck. Peter started sinking, and he was unable to walk on the water anymore. What had gone wrong? Well the scripture said he looked away from Jesus and looked at the massive waves and the strong wind blowing around him, and he started to sink. He started to doubt. He started to walk by sight instead of by faith. He also started to fear. There's two contaminated seeds showing up. The seed of doubt and the seed of fear.

Fortunately Peter cried out; "Lord, save me." Jesus stretched out His hand and caught Peter, picked him up out of the water, and put him right beside Himself. Isn't it awesome to know that when we exercise our faith and we mess up, we have a Savior who will stretch out His hand, catch us, and lift us out of the danger and calamity? I can see Jesus lifting Peter out of the water and making him stand right next to Him, on the water, saying to him: "Peter, come on, let's walk on the water again. Let's walk together, toward the boat, but this time you let Me hold your hand. You look at Me, not at the storm. You don't hybridize your faith with doubt, with unbelief, or with fear. You stop fearing, and you stop doubting and you start believing you can walk on the water again. You put your faith in Me and let's go calm this storm. Come on Peter let's go, let's walk on the water again."

The Bible does not say that's what happened. I'm paraphrasing my own interpretation of what I think could have happened, and what it could have sounded like. Oh, we serve a mighty God, my dear friends. So why did Peter sink after experiencing the victory of walking on the water? What happened to his faith? Jesus quickly told him what had happened. He said: "Oh you of *little faith, or unbelief, why did you doubt*?" Jesus was basically saying to Peter, "Peter, why on earth did you hybridize your faith with little faith, with unbelief. (Remember that little faith is the same as unbelief). "Peter, why did you take *unbelief and doubt* and hybridize it with your faith? What were you thinking? It nullified and weakened your faith so that your faith stopped working and that's why you sank. You had the victory and lost it because you allowed those two contaminated seeds to interbreed and hybridize with your faith, making your faith weak and powerless."

28

Can you imagine the lecture Jesus was giving Peter on hybridized faith? Guys, when we take unbelief or doubt it doesn't matter which one, and hybridize them with our faith, these seeds will destroy the power of our faith. That's how we can also sink into our own storms as well. Come on, let's be honest; how many times have we received victory in healing, or victory in our marriage, or we've stopped smoking, and many more. Then the moment that a symptom appeared and came back, the urge to smoke came back, or maybe the urge to run to the drugs and alcohol came back again, and we started doubting. Unbelief set in. We started fearing and we stopped believing that we were going to be able to stand strong and overcome the attack. Before we even realized what was going on, we were busy sinking and the problem or habit consumed us again. This happened because we hybridized our faith with doubt, unbelief and fear.

All our efforts felt wasted and we we're back smoking, back drinking, and back feeling sick all over again. That's how we sink into the storm instead of walking on top of the storm. That's when the devil tells us those stinking lies that he uses on every one of us. He wants us to believe that our faith is not working. He knows very well that his contaminated seeds of unbelief, fear and doubt have infiltrated and hybridized with our faith, and that our faith has weakened and stopped working like it should work. He knows that we're going to sink because of the hybridizing of our faith. We'll have to counter act these attacks from Satan. Let's get that unbelief and doubt out of our faith life. Don't hybridize your faith with those seeds, please. It's not worth it.

The third example of a bad seed hybridizing with our faith involves fear—a liar by itself. We've already touched on fear when Peter sank after walking on the water because of fear, unbelief and doubt, but let's look at it in detail. Fear tells you that you'll have to be afraid of a situation in your life because you can see what the problem is, and you can see how destructive it's going to be. So you look at the problem, and you start fearing the consequences. But remember what faith says: "Yes, I can see what's going on, but I'm not going to function or live by what I see. I'm not going to let the problem rule over me and consume me. No, I'm going to function by what I've heard the Word of God says about the problem, not by what I'm seeing. I'm going to believe the Word of God instead of what the spirit of fear is showing me." You let the spirit of fear know that you're going to walk by faith, not by sight, according to 2 Corinthians 5:7. That's victory right there, my friend. Rebuke and break the power of the spirit of fear quickly and replace it with the spirit of faith. Let's see how fear contaminates our faith and what the effect of it is when we hybridize it with our faith:

> And suddenly a great tempest (a great storm) arose on the sea, so that the boat was covered with the waves. But He was asleep. Then His disciples came to Him and awoke *Him*, saying, "*Lord, save us! We are perishing!*" But He said to them, "*Why are you fearful, O you of little* faith?" Then He arose and rebuked the winds and the sea, and there was a great calm.

> —Matthew 8:24–26, emphasis mine

In this scripture another storm arose while Jesus was sleeping in the boat. Instead of using their faith and speaking to the storm to go away, the disciples *feared*. Fear immediately hybridized with their faith and took away the power of their faith, weakened it so that it could not function. Their faith was nullified and neutralized immediately by this contaminated lying seed of fear. Jesus addressed this right after they had woken Him up. Again He said to them; *"Why are you fearful, O you of little faith?"* (or you of unbelief). My friends, just like Peter who looked at the waves and the wind and became fearful, started doubting, and then allowed unbelief into his heart and sank into the sea, we find the disciples making the same hybridizing mistake.

They saw this great storm coming, and even with Jesus in the boat with them, they still hybridized their faith with fear and unbelief. It neutralized the power of their faith immediately so that it could not work. I would have thought that they might have learned a lesson by now and reasoned among themselves that they would show Jesus that they had faith that worked. They should have rebuked the storm in faith with no fear at all. Nope, they let fear and unbelief break through and be hybridized with their faith. I want to give you a little nugget here. I've realized that if we as children of God allow it, *"the **spirit of fear can break** our faith."* But, if we don't allow fear to work, but we allow faith to work, *"then our **faith will break** the spirit of fear."* I hope you get this. Read this again and let it sink in! If we as children of God allow it, *"the **spirit of fear <u>can break</u>** our faith."* But, if we allow faith to work *"our **faith <u>will break</u>** the spirit of fear."*

Well, did you understand the lesson on hybrid faith in the boat when Jesus spoke to the disciples? Did you hear the words of Jesus? "Hey people, why are you afraid? Why are you mixing your faith with fear again? Don't you believe that your faith could have calmed the storm? So all you disciples feared and you functioned in unbelief. You woke Me up, and you hit the panic button again. You demonstrated little faith, guys. You're functioning in *unbelief* and in *fear* once again. I thought that you would have learned from the mistakes that Peter had made." I'm sure that Jesus was talking to them in that gentle but instructive tone of voice. Jesus got up and demonstrated the real kind of faith that was not hybridized faith. He rebuked the storm, and there was an immediate calmness because Jesus had no fear, no doubt and no unbelief hybridizing with His faith while addressing the storm. What a faith lesson from Jesus. Shouldn't we be functioning in that kind of faith?

Now listen, these other seeds will come our way. Fear will come to attack us. Unbelief will stick out its neck, and doubt will definitely show up some time or another. The devil will offer them to us on a silver platter every day of our lives so that we'll have the opportunity to hybridize them with our faith. He knows it'll stop our faith from working. He knows it nullifies the power of our faith. He knows it weakens our faith so that it won't work like it should be working and no results are produced. That's part of how the enemy comes to steal, kill, and destroy. (John 10:10)

I believe that Satan will doing everything possible to keep us in that hybridized faith position while we're waiting, and waiting for the miracles that never seem to come. In the meantime it's not God's fault. It's our fault because we're the ones busy hybridizing our faith and that's what's keeping the miracles away, and that's what's stopping us from receiving our victories. We've seen this in the above mentioned examples. Hybridized faith is not going to work when it's crossbred, inter-bred, and contaminated with the seeds of the enemy. I honestly think that we'll start seeing more miracles happening if we can stop this hybridizing process of our faith with the contaminated seeds coming from the devil. I'm one hundred percent sure of that.

CHAPTER 4

What Is Mustard Seed Faith?

The million-dollar question is this: if hybridized faith doesn't work, then what kind of faith does work? Well let's go back to our scriptures that we've already used and see what kind of faith works. According to the scriptures and what Jesus said, it's *mustard seed faith* that works! That's the kind of faith that we need, that kind of faith will cause miracles to take place. Through this kind of faith we're going to be healed, delivered and become prosperous. When we function in mustard seed faith, that's when Jesus is going to say: "Your faith has healed you. According to your faith you are healed." "Are you sure Hansie?" you may ask. Yes, I'm sure. Let me show you what mustard seed faith can do, and what it looks like. First example: We're looking at the epileptic boy again.

> "Lord, have mercy on my son, for he is an epileptic and suffers severely; for he often falls into the fire and often into the water. So I brought him to Your disciples, *but they could not cure hi*m." Then

Jesus answered and said, "O faithless and perverse generation, how long shall I be with you? How long shall I bear with you? Bring him here to Me." And *Jesus rebuked the demon*, and it came out of him; and the child was cured from that very hour. Then the disciples came to Jesus privately and said, "Why could we not cast it out?" So Jesus said to them, *"Because of your unbelief*; for assuredly, I say to you, *if you have faith as a mustard seed, you will say to this mountain, 'Move from here to there,' and it will move*; *and nothing will be impossible for you*. However, this kind does not go out except by prayer and fasting."

—Matthew 17:15–21, emphasis mine

Let's study the scripture of the epileptic boy again. Remember that Jesus was teaching His disciples that faith, hybridized with *unbelief*, does not work. That's why they couldn't heal the epileptic boy, it was because of their *unbelief*. They had hybridized their faith with unbelief. In the same scripture Jesus told them exactly what kind of faith would have worked. He told them: "for assuredly, I say to you, if you have *faith as a mustard seed*, you will say to this mountain, 'Move from here to there,' and it will move; and nothing will be impossible for you." Here comes the truth, guys. *Mustard seed faith* is the only kind of faith that gets results and that works. Mountains will move and nothing will be impossible for us when we use faith as a mustard seed.

35

Okay, so when our faith is hybridized with contaminated seeds from Satan, it doesn't work. We got that! But when we use mustard seed faith, then our faith will work? You bet it will work! Jesus said that when we use mustard seed faith we can speak to the mountain, and it will move to where we tell it to go. Even better than that, nothing will be impossible for us. So if the disciples had used mustard seed faith, then they would've been able to have healed the epileptic boy, right? Yep you are right, that's what Jesus was teaching and explain to them. Praise the Lord. Jesus said if we use our faith like a mustard seed, that's when miracles are going to happen. The mountains in our lives will be removed if we can function with mustard seed faith. That means that sickness mountains, poverty mountains, addiction mountains, anger mountains, and all other mountains blocking us from receiving a victory have to move when we use mustard seed faith. Isn't that incredible? Unfortunately, the opposite is true as well. They won't move if we use hybridized faith.

Here's another example of mustard seed faith. Remember when the disciples asked Jesus to increase their faith, to give them more faith.

> And the apostles said to the Lord, *"Increase our faith."* So the Lord said, *"If you have faith as a mustard seed, you can say to this mulberry tree, 'Be pulled up by the roots and be planted in the sea,' and it would obey you.*

—Luke 17:5, 6, emphasis mine

36

The disciples wanted more faith. Jesus told them plainly that they didn't need more faith; they needed mustard seed–size faith, the smallest seed on the earth. Jesus told them that just a small amount of faith, the size of a mustard seed, had nuclear power. Nevertheless, that was not all that He was referring to. He said they needed faith *as* a mustard seed, actually referring to the size, but also to the purity and power of the mustard seed, which we're going to explain shortly. Nevertheless, the tiniest amount of faith, faith the size of a mustard seed, could accomplish miraculous things Jesus said. He told them in the above scripture that if they had faith, the size of this little mustard seed, they could tell a sycamore tree, called a mulberry tree, to be uprooted and be planted into the sea, and that the tree would listen to them and obey them. That's real faith power right there guys.

For the interest sake a sycamore tree, or a black mulberry tree, grows about twenty to thirty feet tall and has black, juicy berries. This tree has an extensive, deep root system and to pull it up would be a major operation. Jesus said that only a little bit of faith, the size of a mustard seed, could uproot this tree and even uproot mountains. He was encouraging them by saying, "Come on guys, don't stress about more faith, only use the little bit of faith the size of a mustard seed that you possess; that's enough." So these mountains and trees, representing all the problems, troubles, attacks, tribulations, calamities, sicknesses, and trials that the enemy brings our way can be uprooted and be removed through mustard seed faith, even if they are deeply rooted in our lives with a deep root system. Yes, only a small tiny bit of faith is enough to remove these obstacles in our lives, that's incredible! Hybridized faith cannot do that, only mustard seed faith can!

Okay, so faith the size of a mustard seed is what works. That's the kind of faith that plucks up trees and mountains and removes them, not hybridized faith. That's the kind of faith that works and nothing will be impossible for us. That's the kind of faith that we need and that works. That's excellent news and we should be functioning in and through this mustard seed faith, not hybridized faith, I hope you're getting this.

Before I explain the most important fact about mustard seed faith, let me explain something that many of you might have seen, and many may not have seen. Before we move on, you may have a question or two like I had concerning the size of the mustard seed. A mustard seed is little, the tiniest seed on the earth, right? We all know that by now. So, when we use mustard seed faith, we only need a little bit of faith to get results; even though it's so tiny and so small, it still works. That's what Jesus was trying to explain to the disciples. All of a sudden something did not seem right to me. Many people have spoken about the size of the mustard seed. Countless preachers have preached on the mustard seed's size. It's the tiniest seed, so small you can hardly see it or hold it. If we could only have that little bit of faith, we've all preached, that's when miracles would happen. Healings would take place. We've been told this from the pulpit for many years. Guess what; it's all true. We only need that little bit of faith, the size of a mustard seed; that's enough faith to move the mountains and root up trees. So we agree that the size of the mustard seed is powerful. Nevertheless, I was puzzled by what Jesus had told the disciples. Listen to this. Many times in the scriptures that we've used above, when things went wrong and did not work out for the disciples, Jesus would say to them; "*Oh you of __little faith__*." We find some examples in the following scriptures: first, when the disciples could not heal the epileptic young boy:

> So Jesus said to them, "Because of your *unbelief; (little faith)* for assuredly, I say to you, if you have faith as *a mustard seed*, you will say to this mountain, "Move from here to there," and it will move; and nothing will be impossible for you.
>
> —Matthew 17:20

The second example is when Peter sunk into the water after walking on the water: "And immediately Jesus stretched out His hand and caught him, and said to him, "O *you of little faith*, why did you doubt" (Matthew 14:31)? The third example was when they woke Jesus up because a storm was coming, and they were all on the boat: Matthew 8:26 says: "But He said to them, 'Why are you fearful, O you of *little faith*?' Then He arose and rebuked the winds and the sea, and there was a great calm."

Jesus was telling them the whole time that their problem was that they had "*little faith*." He kept on mentioning, "*Oh you of little faith*." I don't know if you got hold of this; there could be confusion for some of us, but not for Jesus. He told them that their *little faith* was their problem, right? That's the reason why they couldn't function by faith, and why their faith was not working, they had little faith? Then Jesus turned around and told them that what they really needed was faith the size of a mustard seed—which is *little faith*. This doesn't make sense, right? Like I always say when I'm preaching; "*Little faith is mustard seed faith*." How can their problem be: "Oh *you of little faith*," and then the answer be: "*You need mustard seed faith*," which is the tiniest *little faith* that there is. This was a bit confusing for me.

It's like someone telling me that they're thirsty all day long and asking me what they should do about it. Well, I'd ask them how much water they drink a day, and the answer could be: "I drink one glass of water per day and I'm still thirsty" Well, let's say I answered them in this way: "That's your problem. You're only drinking one glass of water a day. You need to drink eight ounces of water a day, that's going to solve your problem." If I answered them in that manner, most of you would laugh and say that that's ridiculous Hansie. One cup of water is eight ounces of water. I know. How can you tell someone that their problem is drinking one glass of water, but that the answer to the problem is to drink eight ounces of water. It's the same thing! You see the confusion. That's what Jesus was doing. He told them that their problem was *little faith*, but that the answer was to use *mustard seed faith* (which *is the tiniest faith, little faith*). So replace *little faith* with *little faith*. Did not make any sense to me.

So I looked up the word *little* in the Greek. Now we know that Jesus was definitely not confused, and He was not trying to confuse either His disciples or us. What was Jesus actually saying when He said, "*Oh you of little faith*"? The word "little" in the Greek is *oligo*. It means lacking faith, little faith, unbelief, faith for a short while, skeptical faith, hesitant faith, suspicious

40

faith, questioning faith, and uncertain faith. It means to have anxiety in a situation instead of believing or having faith. To my surprise, it really has nothing to do with size. Little faith does mean small faith, yes, but not in the above verses spoken by Jesus. That's when I realized that Jesus was not saying that they had a problem with little faith in size, but that they were *lacking faith*. He was telling them that they had *unbelief*; that their *faith was of a short duration*. They had a certain amount of *anxiety* instead of faith, that their faith was a *skeptical, hesitant faith, suspicious*, and *uncertain* faith. They were not sure what they were believing, that's what Jesus was talking about when He said ; "*Oh you of little faith*." Why? The reason being that they had mixed their faith, crossbred and hybridized it with fear, doubt, and unbelief. In the above scriptures; "Oh you of little faith" was referring to unbelief most of the times, not faith in size. That made more sense to me. So just to clarify it one more time. Mustard seed faith is definitely powerful because of its size and we only need that little bit of faith to live by, and to get great results from. Nevertheless, in the above verses little faith means much more than only the size of the mustard seed.

Next question. Can we have a lot of faith, big faith? Oh yes, of course, if you want to have a lot of faith, get more faith. Get into the Word of God, read it, do it, study it, and speak it. It will create faith. The Bible says in Romans 10:17: "So then faith comes by hearing, and hearing by the Word of God." So you go get more faith if you want to, but you really only need that little size of a mustard seed faith to get saved, healed, delivered, and to be prosperous and to get results. So what is "*great faith*"? Now, just for the interest sake, remember in the first chapter we spoke about the centurion and the woman from Canaan who asked Jesus to heal and deliver his servant and deliver her daughter? Jesus told them; "Oh woman, *great is your faith*, let it be as you desire." Then to the centurion, Jesus said, "Assuredly I say to you, I have not found such *great faith* not even in Israel." The word *"great"* in the Greek actually means to have large faith, strong faith, mighty faith—more faith than most other people have. It means powerful faith. It means to go from great, to greater, to the greatest faith, from weak to being stronger to the strongest in our faith. Great faith actually leans more towards the power and strength of our faith, than the size of being big faith. This totally helped me so much with the confusion I had concerning *"great faith."*

We don't need a lot of faith, only faith the size of a mustard seed. Nevertheless, we can have great faith, powerful, strong, mighty, large faith, even more faith, if we want it. The *"great faith"* that Jesus spoke about concerning the centurion and the Greek woman was faith that was full of power, might, and strength. That was the kind of faith that they had demonstrated. It was not the size of their faith. It was not how much faith they had, or the amount of faith they had, but rather how powerful their faith was.

Okay, so we all understand that there is power in the size of the mustard seed, right? But, is the power of the mustard seed only in its size? Are there any other characteristics about the mustard seed that made Jesus refer to it as the faith that we should be using. What is it about mustard seed faith that makes it move mountains and get results? Why can mustard seed faith create miracles and healings? I had to find out more about the mustard seed. To my greatest surprise, what I was about to find out was nothing new to mankind. It was all over the internet and in books where anyone could go and look it up and discover all the wonderful characteristics of the mustard seed. I don't think a lot of people ever thought that there was more information about the mustard seed, and they just ignored it. Not a lot of believers have ever heard about this truth about the mustard seed and how powerful it really is. No wonder Jesus used it as an example to be used in our faith lives. So let's explore and find out more!

Now remember, I don't want you to forget this. Jesus told the disciples to use faith like a mustard seed many times while He was teaching them. That was the kind of faith that He wanted them to use because it would move mountains and it created results. The reason He told them to have faith as a mustard seed was because it was so little in size, but also because it had so much power in it. If it was so small and still gave the results that was needed, what else empowered this mustard seed to make it so powerful?

CHAPTER 5

The Power of the Mustard Seed

I'm sure Jesus must have known that there was more to the mustard seed than just the power of its size. The mustard seed had to have a hidden power somewhere because Jesus was hammering it home to the disciples all the time: "if you have faith like a mustard seed." Over and over, again and again, He kept on reminding them. Even the people back then must have known what Jesus was talking about, or they would have asked Him why He kept on mentioning the mustard seed as an example of faith, and not another seed. Why did Jesus not say that we should use grape seed faith, or olive leaf seed faith? Why mustard seed faith? I think they all knew exactly why Jesus was saying have faith as a mustard seed.

Well, don't let me keep you waiting. This is what I found out about the mustard seed and why Jesus was emphasizing "faith like a mustard seed" so many times? Do you remember when we spoke about seeds or animals being crossbred, interbred, or hybridized in the previous chapters? We used an apple seed and an orange seed that was hybridized and we called it an "orple." We spoke about dogs being crossbred as well. The German shepherd and the Great Dane and we got a "Great Shepherd." People are hybridizing seeds and animals all over the world, so they can find out what mixed or hybridized results they can dish up. Now listen to this great news! This is where the real power of the mustard seed is going to be made clear to all of us. Here we go!

Did you know that a mustard seed is the only seed in the plant world that you cannot hybridize or crossbreed with any other seed? Oh, you can try to crossbreed it, and people have tried it, but there are no hybridized results. The mustard seed is so pure and so powerful that if you hybridize it with any other seed, with an apple seed, a broccoli seed, an orange seed, or with any other seed, guess what: the end result will always be mustard. You won't get an apple that's full of mustard or broccoli that is yellow and tastes like mustard. No, the apple seed, broccoli seed, or any other seed that you try and hybridize with the mustard seed is always going to be destroyed by the mustard seed. You will always end up getting mustard as an end result. No hybridizing can take place with the mustard seed. The mustard seed is too powerful for hybridizing to take place. You cannot hybridize any seed with the mustard seed. Let me emphasize the reason why, again: any other seed that you try to hybridize with the mustard seed will be destroyed by the power of the mustard seed. The mustard seed will kill and destroy the apple seed, orange seed, broccoli seed and all the other seeds that we try to hybridize with it. It's too powerful and too pure to be hybridized. Isn't that incredible? That's the power of the mustard seed.

So why will the end result will always be mustard? Well, the pureness and the power of the mustard seed is so powerful, and that's what destroys and kills the other seeds that you are trying to hybridize it with. Oh my goodness. The light just went on in my mind when I read this. I felt like shouting like a Texan: "Ye ha!" No wonder Jesus told the disciples, and us, to have mustard seed faith. He knew that we only needed the size of the mustard seed, yes, but He also knew that we needed the power and the purity of the mustard seed that was available to be used. What a great God we serve! God explained it to me like this:

You see, in reality, when the seed of fear, the seed of doubt, the seed of unbelief, or any other contaminated seed from the devil shows up and it wants to hybridize with our faith. Guess what happens?: if we have mustard seed faith, and we're using our faith like a mustard seed, the hybridizing won't work. Our mustard seed faith will be so strong, so pure, and so powerful that it will destroy the seeds of fear, doubt, anger, unbelief, and all the other contaminated seeds coming from the enemy. The end result will always be mustard seed faith. Mustard seed faith cannot be hybridized with fear, doubt, unbelief, anger, discouragement etc. It's too powerful and will destroy all of these seeds when trying to hybridize them. That's how mustard seed faith moves mountains and trees and we are healed, set free, saved, and delivered because of our faith. Why am I saying contaminated seeds from the enemy? Well, the seeds of fear, doubt, unbelief, anger, hatred, jealousy, stress, worry, unforgiveness, and even anxiety seeds are sent by Satan to contaminate and weaken our faith.

They come to hybridize and nullify the power of our faith. Nevertheless, if we function with faith like a mustard seed they can't hybridize. Mustard seed faith will destroy these seeds and stay pure and powerful and produce results. Incredible!

Satan's aim is still to steal, kill, and destroy — remember; John 10:10. If the devil can contaminate our faith and hybridize it with his contaminated seeds, then our faith will be stolen, weakened, and will most probably not work. We'll have faith, but it'll be idle faith; it'll just be there, existing, faith without power. Our faith will be neutralized. The hybridizing is what weakens the power of our faith, and we'll sink in the storm like Peter did. The lie of the enemy will be that our faith will eventually work; don't worry. Someday it'll break through. He's a liar and a thief. Satan wants to keep us believing that the faith we have is still going to work, someday, not today, sorry, but it's most probably never going to work and the enemy knows that — not if it's hybridized with his fear, doubt and unbelief. It's going to be the pure, powerful mustard seed faith that will destroy the devils contaminated seeds. That's the kind of faith that works, and that we need to function in.

Now listen to me. Unfortunately, like I've already said; fear, doubt, unbelief, and all the other contaminated seeds from the devil will come. They will show up when we least expect them. They will come to attack our faith, and to try and hybridize with our faith. These seeds will always show up, over and over, never ending. Why? They want to steal the power of our faith and weaken it. They come to hybridize our faith so that our faith won't work and we'll sink and give up. Nevertheless, it's how we handle this attack and attempt of hybridizing on our faith that is important. Remember

47

that Satan knows that hybridized faith cannot work, don't be mistaken about that. Where does that leave us? Do we know how to stop and counter attack the hybridizing process? We're going to found out soon.

So the first characteristic of a mustard seed is that it's more pure and powerful than any other seed. When you hybridize it, it destroys the other seed, and mustard is the only end result. The second characteristic of a mustard seed is this: Mustard seeds will only take out the nutrients they need to grow; they don't take anything else out of the soil. They also grow to be a huge tree. The mustard seed is not afraid of anything surrounding it or growing close to it. It does not accept any viruses from any other kind of plants. It refuses all viruses, and there is no way you can make it anything other than what it is: a mustard tree or a mustard plant. It always stays pure and clean and powerful. It always produces pure mustard, nothing else. It does not mix with any other seeds, like we've explained. It can't be hybridized. It grows where other plants will not grow. It can grow in the desert, good ground, even swamps— mostly anywhere you plant it. It has deep root systems. It's a powerful pure seed.

So if I got this right, then the mustard seed faith that we should be using in our daily lives is far more powerful than just the power in its size. All the above characteristics of the mustard seed should be working when we apply our faith like a mustard seed. Our faith should be overpowering all the other contaminated seeds from the devil. Our faith should be so strong that it will never give up and never accept defeat. The roots of our mustard seed faith should be standing strong and should not be moved. These root should be rooted deep into God's Word, being unmovable. Our faith should work and grow in all situations, in any ground, and we should not let any attack weaken it or stop it from working. Our faith should even grow while we're going through the trials and tribulations coming against us. Nothing should be able to cripple or destroy our faith. Our faith should overcome and become more mature in any situation that we go through. That's the powerful mustard seed faith that we should be using. This great truth about the power of the mustard seed has always been there, but very few knew about it. Now that we know the truth, there are no more excuses. We can, and should be making our faith work, so that we can get the results that we need. If we can only stop the hybridizing factor, that's our big challenge.

CHAPTER 6

Releasing Your Mustard Seed Faith

Now that we know that it's only mustard seed faith that works because it cannot be hybridized with any other seed from the enemy, how do we use mustard seed faith instead of hybridized faith? Don't forget that it's possible for any believers faith to be hybridized with fear, doubt, unbelief, anger, hatred, unforgiveness, and so forth, that's if we allow it to be hybridized. That's why Jesus kept on reminding us to have faith like a mustard seed and He kept on saying; "don't be afraid, don't have unbelief, why did you doubt?" He wanted us to function in pure mustard seed faith, not hybridized faith.

As we stated in an earlier chapter, when you hybridize something, it's empowered by two power sources, working together. The faith that Jesus was talking about was the real faith, mustard seed faith, which cannot be hybridized and only has one source of power, the Word of God. Now once again, remember that we're talking about, and working with two kinds of faith: hybridized faith and mustard seed faith. How do we release and use either one of these kinds of faith? How do they work? Firstly, it doesn't matter which kind of faith we're functioning in, the power of either one of them will be released through our mouths. We'll either speak hybridized faith, or we'll speak mustard seed faith. How does that work? The Bible says in Romans 10:17: "So then faith comes by hearing, and hearing by the Word of God." So in other words, whatever we read or listen to, or hear, will go into our ears, it will then be received by our spirit man and will then be released through our mouths. That's how we're going to release either hybridized faith or mustard seed faith. It's spoken. Is this important? Oh yes it is. We have to watch out what kind of faith-filled words we're going to speak, and what kind of words are going to come out of our mouths. Remember that in Mark 11: 23, Jesus said that we can have what we say. So it's important to watch out what comes out of our mouths.

Let's look at an example of hybridized faith. When releasing hybridized faith words, this is most probably what we'll sound like: "I'm always feeling sick; this pain just never goes away. Nothing seems to be going my way. My finances are not working out. All these attacks just never stop, or go away. My back is killing me. I'm so sick and tired of my children being on drugs. These kids make me so nervous. My husband will most probably never get saved, he's too old. It doesn't look like God's going to save or heal my family. It's just my bad luck, I never have good luck you know! I wonder why God's taking so long to heal my mother. Maybe it's His will for me to suffer and have cancer. Sometimes I wonder if God's even hearing my prayers," and so forth and so forth. These are examples of hybridized

51

faith-words spoken, and these word are compared to being foolish in the Bible. Proverbs 18:7 says; "*A fool's mouth is his ruin, And his lips are the snare of his soul.*" When we speak these hybridized words we're snaring ourselves and acting foolish. We're not giving ourselves any chance of being blessed or healed. We're speaking ourselves into the snare and trap of the enemy. Not a good way for believers to speak or believe. I hope you're agreeing with me?

So here we have believers that are believing that God can heal, save, and deliver them, but their mouths are saying that they're afraid and doubting that it's never going to happen. This is the junk that Satan put's into the minds of believers and then it's spoken out of their mouths. These kind of faith-filled words spoken, are obviously hybridized with the contaminated seed of fear, doubt, unbelief, and many other contaminated seeds from the enemy. We speak Gods promises, but then immediately nullify and cancel it with negative words right after we've spoken the truth. These kinds of faith-filled words spoken will make us sink like Peter did. We'll sink and never be able to receive or maintain the miracle of walking on the water because our faith has been hybridized. These words snare us and won't produce any results because they are hybridized.

The opposite of hybrid faith, of course, is mustard seed faith. What does that sound like? Mustard seed faith words, are words spoken that are pure faith-filled words direct from the Word of God. These words are the power source that produces mustard seed faith. It sounds like this: "Thank You Jesus I'm healed, I'm an overcomer. Situations will change in my life, they are going to change. I am going to have victory of these attacks. My husband will get saved, and he will be delivered. I am not afraid, my miracle is coming. My wife will walk again. I will get through these trials and tribulations. I can do all things through Christ Jesus which gives me strength. I will make it through this attack. My son will be set free from drugs, I have no doubt even if I can't see it yet. I'm not giving up. The Word of God says He's my Healer, my Savior, my Deliverer and my Fortress. I'm holding on to His promises. I will prosper in all things; spiritually, emotionally, financially and physically. My marriage will be healthy. I will not die but live and declare the works of the Lord." I can carry on and on, but I think you're getting the point. Hybridized faith is when we're speaking negative words, speaking death. Mustard seed faith, is when we're speaking the Word of God, speaking the Truth, speaking life. What a vast difference in the power of these words.

> *Death and life are in the power of the tongue*, And those who love it will eat its fruit.
>
> —Proverbs 18:21, emphasis mine

"So how do we get mustard seed faith and how do we use it so that it works," you may ask? Well, we know how to get hybridized faith working. Just hybridize your faith with fear, doubt, unbelief, anger, bitterness, and more, and then speak it out of your mouth and see the end results, it's not going be good, right? Now let's see how we can get mustard seed faith. What do we do? Well, we have to do the opposite to hybridized faith and speak pure life words, the Word of God, healing words, words of deliverance. Then we have to believe that what

53

we've said, we can receive. I'm emphasizing this guys, mustard seed faith is speaking life, not death. Actually, all believers should refuse to speak anything else but life, in other words nothing else but God's promises in His Word. That's how pure mustard seed faith is produced, and how it works, by speaking God's promises in His Word.

I'm saying it again, we cannot afford to allow our faith to be hybridized with any of the devil's contaminated seeds my friends. It's not going to work, and all that's going to happen it that our faith will be weakened and we'll become double-minded, discouraged and defeated believers. We'll be Christians believing God for all our needs to be met, but then turn around and speak words filled with doubt, fear and unbelief. We'll believe that God's going to perform miracles, but at the same time we'll also be thinking that He won't perform them. Which one of the two situations do we actually believe? No, let's make up our minds and speak what we want God to do for us. Then, let's believe that God will do it by using our mustard seed faith. Let's believe that He's going to answer our prayers and perform the miracles. "But how can you say that a person must speak that they're healed, when they're not feeling healed and when they cannot see that they're healed?" That doesn't make sense, does it? Well, that's how pure powerful mustard seed faith works. Mustard seed faith is speaking what you expect God can do, what you've asked Him to do, what you want Him to do, and then accepting that He's going to do it. You believe that it's a done deal and that you're going to receive your miracle, that's it. No doubt, no fear, no unbelief, period! Then you thank God for the miracle even though you cannot see it yet, or feel it. That's faith, that's what mustard seed faith is and how it works. That's why it brings forth results. It actually works like this: When we release God's Word, mustard seed faith is produced. Then, that mustard seed faith becomes the substance of the things that we hoped for, or expected God to do for us. It becomes the evidence of things we don't see it yet. That's faith!

> Now *faith is the substance of things hoped for*, the *evidence of things not seen*.
>
> —Hebrews 11: 1, emphasis mine

Mustard seed faith is also calling those thing which are not as if though they are. God did it; so we can do it.

> (As it is written, "*I have made you a father of many nations*") in the presence of Him whom he believed—God, who gives life to the dead *and calls those things which do not exist as though they did*.
>
> —Romans 4: 17, emphasis mine

Mustard seed faith is not looking at the problem, it's looking toward God, the answer. Mustard seed faith is believing that God will supply every need that we have, and accepting that He'll supply those needs without having any fear, doubt or unbelief about it. This is how we walk by faith and not by sight. Mustard seed faith is trusting God, relying on God, and having confidence in God. Mustard seed faith is not looking at what is not working. It's looking at what is going to work; the answer that God has provided, even though we might not be able to see it immediately. It's coming, it's going to happen, and that's how we speak and believe. No fear, no doubt, no unbelief or any other contaminated seed is allowed to hybridize with our faith. That's mustard seed faith in God. "*For we walk by faith, not by sight*" (2 Corinthians 5:7, emphasis mine). You realize that I'm saying mustard seed faith instead of only faith right. The reason why, is that the faith that we should be using should be mustard seed faith. I'm emphasizing it so that every time you see the word faith, or say the word faith, that you'll remember that you're actually meaning pure powerful mustard seed faith. Don't forget that.

Now remember that The Word of God has to be spoken so that we can hear it, again and again. The more we speak the Word of God, the more we hear it, and the more we hear it, the more we'll believe it. That's how faith comes. It goes into our spirit man, out of our mouths, into our ears, and out of our mouths again, over and over. That's what I call the "faith cycle." Does scripture confirm the speaking of our faith-filled words? Yes it does.

> For assuredly, I say to you, *whoever says to this mountain*, 'Be removed and be cast into the sea,' and *does not doubt in his heart, but believes that those things he says will be done, he will have whatever he says*. Therefore I say to you, whatever things you ask when you pray, *believe that you receive them*, and *you will have them*. "And whenever you stand praying, if you have anything against anyone, *forgive him*, that your

Father in heaven may also forgive you
your trespasses. But *if you do not forgive, neither will your Father in heaven
forgive your trespasses.*"

—Mark 11:23–26, emphasis mine

In the above scripture Jesus explains that when we
say, or speak, to the mountain, to the problem, to be
removed and to be cast into the sea, that it will move.
It will listen to us. So when we speak and release faith-
filled words and we speak to the problem, such as a
sickness, addiction, abuse or any other hindrance to go,
it should listen to us, right? Nevertheless, Jesus also
said that we should watch out that we don't hybridize
our faith with doubt when we speak to the problem,
or else our faith won't work. We have to have pure
mustard seed faith, believing that we will receive what
we're saying and what we're asking God to do. That's
when it will be done, and that's when we'll receive
the victory. People have been quoting this scripture
for years and have forgotten about the: "and *does not
doubt in his heart*," part of it. They don't receive what
they have said and wonder why not. Maybe there's been
some faith hybridizing with doubt. Who knows? Let's
check that area of our faith life. No doubting, cut it out
of your faith life.

Then Jesus further explains that whatever we ask
when we pray, we must believe, have faith, that we'll
receive it. That's important. We have to believe that
we're going to receive the healing, the deliverance, or
whatever it is we're trusting God to do. We also have
to believe that when we command the mountain to be
removed that it will move. He then goes one step further

and says that when we stand, praying, or asking God for the miracle, that we must make sure that we don't have unforgiveness in our hearts. In other words, watch out, first of all don't hybridize your faith with doubt, and then secondly, don't hybridize it with unforgiveness. Once again, our faith cannot and won't work if we hybridize it with the seed of doubt or with the seed of unforgiveness. Both of these seeds are contaminating seeds from Satan that will nullify and weaken the power of our faith. We first have to forgive everyone who has done us wrong and hurt us, or God can't forgive us. If we don't forgive, we most probably won't be able to receive the miracle that we've asked for. It's as plain and simple as that. For the first time I'm realizing why many of us are not getting our miracles. We pray, we believe, but nothing happens. In the meantime we're not focusing on the hybridizing aspect of our faith and we think that our faith is not enough, not working, or that God's not answering our prayers. In the meantime we've been missing the whole problem area of hybridizing our faith. We better address this problem.

I urge you again. Let's stop this hybridizing of our faith. I know it's not easy, and no one said it was going to be easy, but man it's worth it. Fear, doubt and unforgiveness and all the other contaminated seeds from the enemy will come, and they will try and contaminate our faith, trying to hybridize it. It does not matter how difficult it might be, we have to break that hybridizing cycle and start speaking only what the Word of God says. We'll have to get all the fear, doubt, unbelief and other seeds out of our lives and refuse to hybridize our faith with them. That's how we're going to generate power to keep our faith pure, and powerful, like a mustard seed.

Now did you realize in Mark 11: 23, the scripture above, that Jesus said speak to the mountain to be removed? He did not say speak about the mountain and say, "Why aren't you going away mountain? Why are you getting bigger? It doesn't seem like I'm going to be able to remove you mountain. Are you going to hinder me for the rest of my life mountain? I'm afraid you're never going to go away mountain, you're too big. Oh my, this mountain is enormous; I wish you would just disappear and go away." When we speak about the mountain in this manner, we're busy hybridizing our faith my friends. Those would be hybrid faith-negative words. No, we don't want to do this. We want to speak to the mountain with faith-filled words of life, believing that it's going to be removed and be cast into the sea. That's mustard seed faith. That's not the way Jesus wanted us to speak.

Hey, sometimes we even pray like this guys: "God I've been praying and I believe that you're hearing me, but nothing is changing or getting better. It's actually getting worse God. It looks like I'll never get through this situation God. Why am I staying sick Lord? When are You going to heal me, God? Can You do something about it Father? This mountain of sickness doesn't look like it's going to be removed. I just can't take this torment anymore Lord. Okay Lord, if it is Your will, will you remove this sickness mountain from me, please Lord I beg You? If it's not Your will then I'll accept the sickness and the pain God." Have you ever prayed a prayer that sounds like the one above? That's totally the opposite what Jesus told us to pray and say in Mark 11: 23. It's absolutely the wrong kind of prayer to pray and the wrong way to speak. Well, you guessed right, that's a hybridized faith prayer that will produce no results at all.

It's sometimes hard not to pray this way, right, when things are going wrong and nothing's changing and the pain and discomfort never let's go, I know; I've been there. When you realize that you're praying the above kind of prayer, hold on; get your mind straight and in line with God's Word. Change your vocabulary. Start speaking and praying life, the Word of God, keep moving forward, not backwards. Even if you're crawling inch by inch, keep going forward toward your promises and miracles in spite of how hard it is and how impossible it looks. Speak that miracle into existence. Declare that it will come to pass, even though you can't see it happening yet. Start thanking God for the miracle. Speak and pray the answer, the healing. Speak healing scriptures or scriptures that talk about your problem. Speak and pray them out loud. Speak to the problem using the Sword of the Spirit, the Word of God. Fight with the power of the Word. It's better than hybridizing your faith and losing your miracle, I hope you're getting this? The above kind of hybridized prayer, or way of speaking was not what Jesus said we should be doing, so let's stop it and change our speech. Let's pray the mustard seed faith prayer instead.

We should rather be using the pure, powerful mustard seed faith that we have received according to the authority and power of God's Word. That's when our faith will rise up, and that's when we'll get results. We need to be walking on top of the storm, not sinking into it. The problem is supposed to be under our feet, we're not supposed to be under the problem's feet. We're the overcomers. So always keep in mind that we can't afford to hybridize our faith, or else we're definitely going to sink into the water, into the problem, and there'll be no victory. Our faith won't work because it'll be contaminated and be weakened because of the hybridized factor.

Let's look at an example of someone who spoke and exercised their mustard seed faith and received their miracle. We pick up the story of the woman with the issue of blood once again. Now remember that she had been sick for twelve years, walking around bleeding every day of her life for twelve years. Oh my goodness, I cannot even image going through such torment. Then, everywhere she went, people would recognize her, and they would chase her away because she was seen as unclean, according to the law of the Old Testament in Leviticus. That's the way it worked in those days. She could go nowhere. She must have heard from someone that if she could get to Jesus that He could heal her. At this stage of her life she must have been a very discouraged but desperate woman. Let's read her story.

> And suddenly, a woman who had a flow of blood for twelve years came from behind and touched the hem of His garment. *For she said to herself, "If only I may touch His garment, I shall be made well."* But Jesus turned around, and when He saw her He said, "Be of good cheer, daughter; your faith has made you well." And the woman was made well from that hour.
>
> —Matthew 9:20–22, emphasis mine

I believe this must be one of the best examples of someone exercising mustard seed faith. Get this picture in your mind: she came to touch the hem of Jesus' garment. She wanted to touch His clothes. Not wanting to be noticed, she came up from behind the Lord. How she got through this crowd of people I don't know. In some places she may have needed to crawl, who knows, but she got to Jesus and touched the border or hem of His garment the Bible says. For the interest sake, the word *border* does not denote a hem or border at the bottom of a man's robe or trousers. What this woman actually touched was the tassels on the corners of Jesus' robe. The outer robe, the cloak, or the mantle that the men wore in those days, was rectangular in shape and had four tassels, one on each corner. They were worn by men in obedience to the injunction of the Law in Numbers and Leviticus. It was so special that the cloak was used to cover the bodies of those who had died. These fringes or tassels represented the totality of the Torah, the Word of God. Each tassel, on each corner of the robe had five double knots each, representing the first five books of the Bible. This is what the woman touched, the tassel, and immediately she was healed. What a reminder to us that we can find deliverance and healing through the Word of God as well. We are able to find victory over impossible situations and attacks when we come to Jesus Christ and give Him authority over our lives. Remember that the God sent His Word and healed us all. (Ps.107: 20)

When she got to the place where Jesus was, there was a multitude of people around Him. Mark 5:27–34 says that people were everywhere. She had no choice but to move through the crowd, between all the people to get to Jesus. The Bible says people were thronging, or crowding Jesus, pressing against Him. They were all around Him, touching Him. She had to make her way through that crowd to get to Jesus which could have caused a lot of problems for her. Can you imagine getting there and seeing all these people? That'll upset and get a person discouraged, right? Nevertheless, she refused to give in and go back home thinking it was not going to work. She decided to go forward towards Jesus, not backwards, giving up.

You think the seed of fear and discouragement did not rise up in her and try to hybridize with her faith? Of course it did. If it was one of us, we most probably would have said: "Oh no man. Just look at the crowd. How am I ever going to get to Jesus? That's just my bad luck again, I might as well go home. I'm never going to get through that crowd and touch Jesus without someone seeing me. And if the people recognize me before I get to Him, they'll most probably send me away before I even get to Him anyway. That's the way it always works, something always goes wrong." That could have been her attitude and she could of given up, hybridized her faith with fear and discouragement and left, like many of us would have done, and she would never have received her healing. Oh no that was not her attitude at all. My friends, this little lady had mustard seed faith. She was not going let any fear, discouragement, anger, doubt, unbelief, or any other seed from Satan hybridize with her faith. No way; she was determined to get healed that day, and she pressed through that crowd, desperate to get healed. Her desperation led her to make a decision, and what a powerful decision she made! Listen to this decision made by this sick woman: "*for she said to herself,*" is what the Bible says. She was not saying to anyone else, no, "*she said to herself, If only I can touch His garment, I shall be made whole*." Isn't that incredible? She had made up her mind and decided what she wanted, and what she was going to do. She spoke it to herself; she spoke life into herself. She refused to hybridize her faith with what she saw. She refused to hybridize her faith with the seed of fear and discouragement coming from the devil and she just went forward, in spite of all the obstacles in her way. In spite of the crowd that blocked her. In spite of what could have happened to her. If the people recognized her they would have sent her away remember! She did not care. She was going to use her mustard seed faith to get healed. And that's what happened. After Jesus had asked who had touched Him, the lady came forward and told Jesus what had happened.

Jesus looked at the woman and said: "*Be of good cheer daughter, your faith has made you well*." If she had hybridized her faith earlier on with fear, doubt, unbelief and discouragement, she would have left without getting healed and with an attitude of: "Oh well, maybe it's just one of those things. All those people are in my way, and I'll most probably never get to Jesus. That's if touching His garment would even heal me." Can you see the lie of hybridized faith? But Jesus nails it on the head when He tells her that her mustard seed faith had so much power that it had made her well; it healed her. He said: "Be of good cheer daughter, *your faith has made you well*." What a victory and what a great miracle, all because she used pure powerful mustard seed faith, and not hybridized faith. She walked away that day healed, immediately, after touching those tassels.

Let me give you some good news today. The speediness of the immediate cure emphasizes the greatness of Jesus' power. Jesus could do in an instant what many doctors had not been able to do in twelve years of treatment. This immediate healing illustrates what happens in the matter of our salvation, our healing and for all of our needs. Evil habits, which people have tried repeatedly to quit, will be quickly conquered when they have come to Jesus Christ for salvation. When Christ saves us, He saves us immediately. When He heals us He heals us immediately. I believe that with all of my heart. When we put our mustard seed faith in Christ, that's when we get healed, saved, and delivered from Satan's bondages—immediately, even if there are still some symptoms left. Now the best news is this: The same immediate power that was used to change this woman's life and heal her, is still the same immediate power that is available today to save us, heal us, deliver us and supply every need that we have as well, immediately!

What a great God we serve and what a great promise we have from God's Word. But, we have to do our part and use our mustard seed faith, not hybridized faith to be able to receive this promise. I want to encourage you to start speaking to yourself, to your body. Start telling yourself that the miracle you're trusting God to do, will come to pass. Then believe that it's going to happen. Start telling yourself that your marriage is going to end up being successful. Tell yourself that your body it's going to be healed. Start speaking to your body, and command it to be healed. Start speaking to yourself about what God has done for you on the cross, and receive it. Can you do that? Of course you can. What was done on the cross by Jesus, was done for all of us. We have to speak and believe it, and then go and claim and receive the salvation, the healing, deliverance, protection, blessings and prosperity in all things, that Jesus died for on the cross. It was promised to us, so let's go get it.

Like I just explained: the cross was for all of us. The blood of Jesus was shed for all of us. His body was beaten for all of us. Our salvation and our healing and all our problems were taken care of on the cross. Let's stop talking about what the devil is trying to do to us. Let's rather start talking about what Christ has already done for all of us on the cross. Speak the answer, not the problem. That's exercising our mustard seed faith.

Man, I'm excited because I can see people getting healed, delivered, getting their finances fixed, marriages restored, and getting free from addictions and bondages because they're living by mustard seed faith. If you get hold of this mustard seed faith truth, you'll start seeing things begin to change. If it doesn't happen immediately, don't get discouraged and go hybridizing your faith again. Keep going forward; never give up. The breakthrough will eventually come, just hold on to God's promises. Remember we're fighting a good fight of faith, it's a battle. It might take some time. There's no red carpet treatment from the enemy. He's apposing every miracle and healing by wanting to hybridize our faith with his contaminated seeds so that we can't receive our blessings and miracles. No, you keep on exercising that mustard seed faith of yours, it will eventually create the results that we need. Remember, hybridized faith does not work and will never work, it produces nothing! Let me show you another scripture to prove it and to remind you of it.

> But let him ask in faith, with *no doubting, for he who doubts is like a wave of the sea* driven and tossed by the

wind. For *let not that man suppose that he will receive anything from the Lord; he is a double-minded man*, unstable in all his ways.

—James 1:6–8, emphasis mine

Are you getting it? Here we go again. If we hybridize our faith with doubt, we will receive nothing from the Lord, because we're double-minded. We have to exercise our mustard seed faith; that's when we'll receive the miracle that we're believing God for. I think our problem is that we've fallen into the habit of using hybridized faith, instead of mustard seed faith and we've never realized it; I know, I've been there. Our mouths have been the key. We've been releasing and speaking hybridized faith words over and over again, instead of speaking and releasing mustard seed faith-filled words through our mouths. Do you realize that even Jesus used mustard seed faith. Did He? Yes, let's see what the scripture says.

Now in the morning, as He returned to the city, He was hungry. And seeing a fig tree by the road, He came to it and found nothing on it but leaves, *and said to it*, "Let no fruit grow on you ever again." Immediately *the fig tree withered away.* And when the disciples saw it, they marveled, saying, *"How did the fig tree wither away so soon?"* So Jesus answered and said to them, "Assuredly, I say to you, *if you have faith and do not doubt, you will not only do what was*

67

done to the fig tree, but also if you say to this mountain, 'Be removed and be cast into the sea,' it will be done. And whatever things you ask in prayer, believing, you will receive."

—Matthew 21:18–22, emphasis mine

Jesus was hungry. He saw a fig tree but it had no fruit on it. What did He do? He spoke to the tree and cursed it. The disciples the next morning thought, wow, how did this tree wither away so quickly? So Jesus taught them another lesson on mustard seed faith. He told the disciples that if they had faith in God, not faith that's hybridized with doubt, that they would be able to do the same as He did. They would even be able to tell a mountain to be removed. The best part is that whatever they asked for in prayer, believing, or having faith that they would receive it, they would actually receive it. The important part here was not to hybridize their faith with doubt. Jesus knew that mustard seed faith would work, and He had set an example for them and for us. When He spoke to the tree He had no fear, no doubt or unbelief. He knew what He had spoken, and He believed that it would happen, and it did. He used pure mustard seed faith. Using mustard seed faith always produces results. So, whatever we ask for in prayer, believing that we will receive it, we actually can receive it if we use mustard seed faith. That's the power of mustard seed faith in working. Come let's do it, guys.

I quickly want to remind you that every time that I speak or mention the words "mustard seed faith" in a sentence, I'm talking about faith-filled words that are not mixed with any fear, doubt, or unbelieving words.

Mustard seed faith is only empowered by the pure Word of God. It's words of life that must be spoken. So don't get confused or forget what it's all about when you read that phrase. It has already been used in the previous chapters, and it'll be used many more times throughout this book. Let's look at the reasons why we have to speak and release our faith-filled words through our mouths.

"Hansie, you keep on saying we have to release and speak mustard seed faith-filled words. Why do we have to speak the Word of God all the times?" That may be a question that you're asking, and not really understanding exactly why we have to speak it. In the next chapter we'll address this question in full but in Isaiah 55: 11 God says; "So shall My word be that goes forth from my mouth; *what I please, And it shall prosper in the thing for which I sent it*." Do you understand this scripture? Go d said that when we return His Word to him that it shall not return to Him void, it's going to accomplish what pleases Him and it's going to prosper in the thing for which He sent it. What did God send His word to do? Palms. 107:20 says that God sent His word and healed us and delivered us from all our destruction. So, if return that word to God it's going to accomplish what He sent it to do. It's going to heal and save us from destruction. That's why we have to return God's Word back to Him by speaking it. I hope this clears up some confusion?

CHAPTER 7

Why Must I Speak My Faith?

It is very important to verbalize our faith. We have to say it; we have to speak faith-filled words. The faith that comes from hearing the Word of God has to be released through our mouths. It's very important to speak what we believe. Why do we have to speak and release our faith through our mouths? Well, it's for our own good. Let me show you what the Word says about it.

> A man's *stomach shall be satisfied* from
> *the fruit of his mouth, From the produce*
> *of his lips he shall be filled.*
>
> —Proverbs 18:20, emphasis mine

What is this scripture saying? Well, first of all, a man's stomach, his belly, is the inner part of a man. The meaning of the word *stomach*, or *belly*, is referring to a man's spirit, the inner man, the mind, his thought life, his spirit man. The scripture is basically saying that our spirit man, our mind, our thought life, our inner man, is

70

going to receive the fruit that comes from our lips, and it will be satisfied with the words that we speak. Our spirit man is going to be filled up, or have enough; it's going to be satisfied with what we've been saying through our mouths. Good or bad words, it doesn't matter. Whether it's right or wrong words, it doesn't matter. Whether it's negative words, or the truth from God's Word, it doesn't matter. Our spirit man is going to be satisfied with whatever words we speak.

This is very important but very dangerous. This is a wakeup call for many believers. If we're speaking words of death, our spirit man is going to be satisfied with those words and receive them. If we're speaking life, then our spirit man is going to be satisfied with the words of life. Which way are you talking? What's your speech like? When we speak with hybridized faith-filled words, or negative words, our spirit man will be satisfied and accept it. When we speak with mustard seed faith-filled words, God's Word, then our spirit man will be satisfied with those words and accept it. I think some of us will have to start changing our vocabulary, quickly! The Amplified Bible explains the same scripture a bit differently:

> A man's [moral] *self shall be filled with the fruit of his mouth; and with the consequence of his words he must be satisfied [whether good or evil].*
>
> —Proverbs 18:20 (AMP),
> emphasis mine

71

The Message puts it this way:

> *Words satisfy the mind* as much *as fruit does the stomach*; good talk is as grati-fying as a good harvest.

> —Proverbs 18:20 (MSG),
> emphasis mine

In both of the translations above, it explains that what we say will satisfy our spirit man, it will infil-trate our minds, and we'll pay the consequences of what we've said, good or bad. It's serious stuff guys, whether we're speaking either hybrid faith-filled words, or mustard seed faith-filled words. I don't know about you, but I don't want my spirit man to be satisfied with words like: "Oh my father died from a heart attack, so I'll most probably have a heart attack. My mother had breast cancer; it's in our family, so I'm just waiting for it to show up in my life. I'm so sick and tired of my life, I just don't know what to do anymore. These kids are driving me crazy. My back is killing me. I'll most probably never get old enough to see my grandchildren, most of my family died early on in their years. I've always got bad luck when I apply for jobs," and that's not all. There's a lot more negative words that we're speaking that's being accepted by our spirit man and by our minds, and it's busy harming us. Can our tongue harm us? Well of course it can. James 3:6 says; "And the tongue is a fire, a world of iniquity. The tongue is so set among our members *that it defiles (contaminates) the whole body* and sets on fire the course of nature; and it is set on fire by hell." (emphasis mine). I don't want my tongue defiling or contaminating my entire body, so that it sets on fire the course of my life, or my existence, or the way that my life is going to end up because of the negative death words that I'm speaking. I don't want those words to satisfy my spirit man. I don't want to speak that I'm going to die early because my grandfather died early. That's changing the course of my life because of the hybridized words that I've spoken. I don't want that kind of life, thank you very much! How about you?

Come on; be honest now. That's the way many of us are talking, and our spirit man is being satisfied with this junk. I told my wife that one day when we ever stop traveling as evangelists, I'm going to open a funeral home right next to a big church of five thousand people or more. I'm going to make a lot of money. All I've have to do is wait for all those Christians who are speaking death, to die. Many of them will die from their backs that are killing them and some will die from laughter. Some are going to die because of their grandchildren that are so cute. Some are just waiting to die because they've just turned fifty, and they believe that they're old, bald and fat, going downhill and waiting to die to go home to Jesus. They're just holding on until Jesus comes, and so forth. You think I'm joking. I hear these words in every church that I preach. I'm not being funny or sarcastic. This might sound funny and even ridiculously insane, but this is the way that many believers are speaking. All you're hearing is death, dying, old, and sickness speech. Are you hearing what I'm saying guys? Christians are speaking these words into their spirit man and their spirit man is being satisfied with these negative words of death. They're speaking death words and not realizing what the effects are going to be, or can be. That's not what Jesus told us to do.

We might think it's not important, but we're speaking and releasing a spirit of death into our lives, into our finances, our bodies, our families, jobs, and a lot of other areas. Instead of speaking life, our spirit man is getting filled up and being satisfied with all those negative, death words that are coming out of our mouths. That's not good, not at all. A child of God should not be speaking hybridized faith-filled words. So how should a child of God be speaking? What does the scripture say? Well, we've said that a child of God must speak mustard seed faith-filled words, the Word of God. We saw what Proverbs 18:20 said in the Old Testament. Let's see what the New Testament says about how a child of God, a believer should be speaking:

> But the *righteousness of faith speaks in this way, "Do not say in your heart, 'Who will ascend into heaven?'* "(that is, to bring Christ down from above)* or, "'Who will descend into the abyss?'* "(that is, to bring Christ up from the dead). *But what does it say? "The word is near you, in your mouth and in your heart"* (that is, the word of faith which we preach): that if you confess with your mouth the Lord Jesus and believe in your heart that God has raised Him from the dead, you will be saved. *For with the heart one believes unto righteousness, and with the mouth confession is made unto salvation.*

—Romans 10:6–10, emphasis mine

Now we all know that when we get saved, we become righteous, right? Everyone who accepts Jesus Christ as Lord and Savior becomes righteous through Christ Jesus who died on the cross, for all our sins, and for all our sicknesses. We cannot make ourselves righteous; only Christ can. The scripture says in 2 Corinthians 5: 21: "For He made Him who knew no sin to be sin for us, *that we might become the righteousness of God through Him*." (emphasis mine).We become righteous through Christ Jesus dying on the cross for us and making us righteous. That's how we're called the righteous. Look at the scripture in Romans 10: 6-10 again: "*The righteousness of faith speaks in this way*." This means that the righteous believers, that's us, people who are saved by faith, this is the way that we should be speaking. This scripture plainly tells us what our speech should be like.

First of all the scripture says that we should not be saying in our hearts: "who will ascend into heaven, or who will descend into the abyss?" By reading these words I understand that we should stop saying and asking the why, the who, the when, and the I don't understand questions. We are so good at it. "Why is God not healing me? Why is it taking so long before He heals me. What is happening? Why do I have to go through all of these trials and tribulations, and so forth?" Speaking with the "why attitude words," is the wrong way of speaking. It is the doubting, unbelieving, full-of-fear way of speaking. It's the hybridized-faith way of speaking.

The scripture further says: "*but what does it say*?" In other words what does the righteous person that is full of faith say. How do they speak? Here comes the answer at the end of the scripture. "*The Word is near*

75

you, in your mouth and in your heart, (that is the word of faith which we preach)." So what I'm getting from this scripture is that we as the righteous believers, we have to speak the Word of God that is in our mouth, and in our heart, (heart meaning; our mind, spirit, thought life, our will, our inner man). Do you see that the Word of God should first be in our mouths, and then be spoken, then our ears will hear it and then it will go straight into our hearts, our spirit man.

The Word of God should be engraved in our minds, our spirit man, our thought life, our will, and our hearts, so that when we open our mouths, the only words that will be spoken, will be the Word of God, the Truth. These faith-filled words are the only words that produce mustard seed faith, and mustard seed faith is the only kind of faith that creates miracles, healings, salvations and deliverances. Mustard seed faith words are the only words that remove mountains. All other words of death that are spoken will create defeat in our lives and weaken our faith. Okay, so now we realize and we accept that we have to speak faith-filled words, because what we say will be received by our spirit man, and our spirit man will be satisfied and be filled by what we say, good or bad.

Now some people might still have a problem with how our spirit man gets satisfied by what we say. So how does our spirit man get the words into it? I love the scriptures because they tell us all that we need to know. I'm so glad that God's whole Word was written down by the disciples, inspired by the Holy Spirit and that it was given to us, so that we can be taught and be instructed by it. Remember the following: We don't receive the promises in the scriptures by knowing that they are written in the Bible. No, we can only receive those promises by speaking them into our hearts, into our spirit man, into our minds, into our thought life, and into our inner man, and then believing these Words that are written in the scriptures. How do we speak them into our hearts? How is God's Word imprinted into our spirit man? Solomon says in Proverbs:

> Let not mercy and truth forsake you;
> Bind them around your neck, *Write*
> *them on the tablet of your heart.*
>
> —Proverbs 3:3, emphasis mine

The Bible says to write mercy and truth on the tablet of our hearts, to bind them around our necks. The Word of God is the truth and should be written on the tablet of our hearts, our spirit man. How do we do that? In the book of Psalms it's explained:

> My heart is overflowing with a good
> theme; I recite my composition con-
> cerning the King; *My tongue is the pen*
> *of a ready writer.*
>
> —Psalm 45:1, emphasis mine

Isn't this neat? The psalmist explains that his heart is full of a good theme. The word *theme* in the Hebrew means a good word, a good saying, a good language. He's saying that his heart, his spirit man, is full of good words toward the king. Then he says that he recites his composition concerning the king. He's actually saying: "I will speak of the things which I have done for the king." He's saying that the deeds and labor that he's done for the king will be spoken out of his mouth. Listen to this. Then he explains how he will do this:? "My tongue is the pen of a ready writer." That's how these words got in to his heart, into his spirit man. He calls his tongue a pen that will write on his heart. It is as simple as that, guys.

Our tongues have to be used like pens. Use that pen to write all the things that God has done for us, what He's promised us in His Word, and what He is still going to do for us; let's write them on our hearts, into our spirit man with our tongues. Those words will be transformed and will produce pure mustard seed faith in our spirits. Our tongues will then speak those faith-filled words. We'll be saying what we've been believing, our ears will hear it, and it'll go back into our spirit man, our hearts. In other words, when we get the Word of God into our hearts, into our spirit man, with our tongues, that's when we speak ourselves healed. That's when we speak ourselves whole, prosperous, set free, and delivered. The faith-filled words released through our mouths will create mustard seed faith which in turn will create results and miracles. That's what happened in the days of Jesus when He was on earth.

Now watch out. Don't be deceived. Never speak anything that disagrees with the Word of God, that won't work. Only words that agree with God's Word will produce mustard seed faith and results. Any other words disagreeing with God's Word are words of doubt, worry, fear, unbelief, discouragement, and more. These words will bring forth hybridized faith, which does not work. We have to always make sure that we focus on how we're speaking, what we're saying. This is very important because it's the difference between getting healed or staying sick, being blessed or being cursed, having victory or having defeat. At this point of time we know this: (1) Faith must be spoken; and (2) We have to speak it to satisfy our spirit man. So now the next question is: "Why do we have to satisfy our spirit man?" What does our spirit man do with what we write on it with our tongues? What happens to our spirit man when it hears what we're saying? Let's find out.

CHAPTER 8

Why Must I Satisfy My Spirit Man?

"**W**hy satisfy our spirit man?" That is a good question to ask. When our spirit man hears the words that come from our mouths, what happens is this: our spirit man gets satisfied with the words that we've spoken. I explained that in the previous chapter. Now, when our spirit man gets filled with the words that we've spoken, what happens next? Let's see what the wise Solomon has to say about it in Proverbs.

> *The spirit of a man will sustain him in sickness, But who can bear a broken spirit?*

> —Proverbs 18:14, emphasis mine

Solomon tells us that the spirit of a man will sustain him when he gets sick. So how does that happen? Well, we have to speak and release faith-filled words into our spirit man so that it can be satisfied with those words that come out of our mouths. That's when our spirit man receives the words that we've spoken and that's when our "*spirit will sustain us in sickness*" or in any calamity. Let's quickly look at the word *sustain*. In the Hebrew language it has a few meanings. It means: "to keep, to hold up, to feed, to nourish, to provide for." So, when we speak the Word of God and we release those faith-filled words through our mouths, our ears hear those words. Those words are then written into our hearts, our spirit man, with our tongues, the pen. When our spirit man receives those mustard seed faith-filled words, then, when the sicknesses, attacks, addictions, worries, stress, anxieties, anger, or any trials or tribulations come, guess what? That's when our spirit man says, "No, we're not going to accept this sickness. No, we're not going to become fearful and worried. We're not going to speak death. We're going to overcome this problem. We are victorious through Christ Jesus. We are children of God. God is our Healer, our Savior, and our Deliverer. God's Word is our power, and it's the truth of God that sets us free. God's Word was sent to heal us. No weapon formed against us shall prosper, and every tongue that rises against us in judgment we shall condemn. Greater is He that is in us than he that is in the world. Greater is God's power and anointing that is in us than the power of the attack that comes from the enemy. We are healed by the stripes of Jesus." That's how our spirit man sustains us, holds us up, provides for us, carries us through the attacks, and keeps us going, believing, never giving up—fighting the good fight of faith.

My dear friends, can you see the significance of filling and satisfying our spirit man with the word of God that produces mustard seed faith. When things start going wrong and the calamities come and we need healing and help, then our spirit man is going to rise up and sustain us, hold us up, and keep us going. Our spirit man is going to provide all the Word, and mustard seed faith that we're going to need to get through these attacks so that we can be victorious in the end. How does our sprit man do this? Well, we've been supplying our spirit man with the Word of God. We've been sowing the seed of the Word into out spirit man. It's full of the Word of God, which is the power of God unto salvation. Romans 1: 16 explains it; " For I am not ashamed of the gospel of Christ, *for it is the power of God to salvation for everyone who believes*, for the Jew first and also for the Greek."

We've spoken the Word of God, which is the power of God into our spirit man, and now our spirit man is strong, powerful and ready to fight because it's filled up with the Word of God. Nothing can stand before the Word of God. No demon, no sickness, not Satan himself, absolutely nothing has the power that is stronger than God's Word. That's why it's so important that we get the Word of God into our spirit man, quickly and continually. Also remember that the Word of God is medicine to our souls. Proverbs 4: 20 says; "My son, give attention to my words; Incline your ear to my sayings. Do not let them depart from your eyes; Keep them in the midst of your heart*; For they are life to those who find them, And health to all their flesh*."(emphasis mine). Doctors give us certain medicines for certain sicknesses and that's great! Nevertheless, God gives us spiritual medicine that we have to take by reading the Scriptures and writing them into our spirit man. The scripture says we have to regularly take these Words of God and then release and speak them, for they are health to our flesh. The Word of God will heal us, that's a fact.

Always remember that the Word of God is the only power source that creates mustard seed faith. Mustard seed faith has no other power source. When the Word of God is written into our spirit man with our tongues, our spirit man takes that Word and transforms it into mustard seed faith. Then when mustard seed faith-filled words are formed and released through our mouths, we're speaking life, wholeness, healing, completeness, deliverance, salvation, and prosperity; that's when we get the victory. That's when miracles start happening. That's how we're healed and made whole by our own faith. That's how the people who got healed in Jesus' time got healed—by their faith, which they spoke through their mouths. That's why Jesus told many of them: "Your faith has healed you." We should be functioning in that same power and same kind of mustard seed faith. You see this makes the spirit of a man joyful and merry, and it's like medicine to a man.

> *A merry heart does good, like medicine,*
> But *a broken spirit dries the bones.*
>
> —Proverbs 17:22, emphasis mine

Nevertheless, the opposite is true as well. If we speak bad news and we fill and satisfy our spirit man with negative words of death, unfortunately, the opposite effect will manifest. Your spirit man will accept those negative words as well. Why? Because we're speaking them into our spirit man, and then, when sickness and calamities come, guess what? When that sickness comes, our spirit man cannot help us, or lift us up, or feed us with the Word of God, or even provide the Word of God because it's not there. We've got nothing to fight with, no weapon, no sword of the Spirit. We've been speaking negative words all the time, instead of God's Word. We don't have God's Word deposited into our spirit man. It was not spoken into our spirit man and we're in trouble. Our spiritual bank account is empty, with no Word in it. The power of God is not in our spirit man. The faith that we have, has been hybridized with fear, doubt, unbelief, anger, unforgiveness, and many other contaminated seeds from the devil. Instead of having pure powerful mustard seed faith, we have hybridized faith, and we know by now that this kind of faith does not work, it does not reproduce anything but trouble and defeat. We become depressed and discouraged. We give up and stop believing because we have a broken spirit and dried up bones. There's no Word in our spirit man to back us up and help us, or sustain us and we're in deep spiritual trouble! We lose our joy, and we think that God does not want to heal us or help us. Meanwhile our spirit man is just acting the way we've been speaking to it. Do these words sound familiar? "Well, it's winter again. I usually get sick every winter you know. I'm just waiting for it to show up. I might as well go to the doctor and get the medicine ahead of time. Do you know, I get the flu every February? You can count on it." Or, "I'll most probably have a heart attack because my father had a heart attack and died from it. My mother had breast cancer so I'll definitely get breast cancer, that's what the doctor says. It's just a matter of time. I got diabetes because it's in my family, I just have to live with it. That's just how life is. There's nothing I can do about it. I'll most probably lose my job too. I'm just like my Dad. I can't keep a job for longer than six months, that's just the way the Smith family works." Oh no it's not! Satan's lying to many of us and deceiving us to believe this nonsense.

What about God's Word? What about praying. What about speaking God's powerful Word. Have we forgotten about the power of the Word of God? Have we forgotten that we can ask in prayer and receive what we believe. Are we believing the report of the devil, are we believing what people are saying, what family members and doctors are saying and ignoring God's report and promises? The Bible is full of God's reports and promises of healing, salvations, success, prosperity, love, care, kindness, and a whole lot of other promises that God has given us. Why aren't we holding on to those words and speaking them? That's why our spirit man has nothing to work with. It has no Word of God to fight with, and automatically agrees and gets satisfied with the negative words of death that we speak. Our spirit man then acknowledges the words that we speak, and when the incidents and attacks show up and it reacts according to the words that we've spoken and it says, "That's what you've been speaking and if that's what you want, that is what's going to happen, there's nothing I can do about it. You asked for the flu and your immune system is not fighting back. You've lost your job because you believed you would." Our poor spirit man has no Word power to help us against the attacks and can't sustain us through the attacks and sicknesses. That's sad that so many believers are caught up in this awful situation.

I don't know about you, but that doesn't work for me. I don't like this outcome. It just doesn't sound right to me, but that's what happens when we speak those kind of words into our spirit man. Are we going to change our way of speaking and start exercising mustard seed faith, or are we going to continue filling our spirits with the devils lies and junk?

So, if I can encourage you today, please stop speaking words of death into your spirit man. Rather start focusing on speaking life, the Word of God, in spite of what you're going through. Speak those words of life during the attack; even if you don't feel healed yet, speak them as much as you can. They are like medicine to your bones. In Psalm 107:7, it says that *"God's Word was sent to heal us all."* Don't let negative death words cause a broken spirit in you, which can cause you to lose your healing, your deliverance, and many other promises in God's Word. Grab hold of God's promises, speak them into your spirit man, believe that you can receive them, and don't stop speaking these precious Words of life. Let your mustard seed faith heal you! Stop using hybridized faith that is mixed with fear, doubt, negative, stressed, and worrisome words.

Okay, Hansie, but what if I've spoken the Word of God as you've explained, and it still doesn't work? That's another good question. If I had the answers to why the victory has not yet manifested or when it is going to happen, I will definitely tell everyone immediately. But I don't know the answer. I don't think anyone on earth can give you a comprehensive answer of why some people get healed immediately and why others get healed later on and why some never get healed and even die. No one knows those answers. At least, if we've been speaking words of life over ourselves and into our spirit man, we've been fighting the good fight of faith, we've not given up, and we're given ourselves a fair chance of being healed. That's when the enemy cannot condemn us that we haven't done all that we could have done. If we've prayed and believed, if we've spoken the Word of God and believed, if we've thanked God ahead of time for the miracle, and we've not given up on receiving God's promises, the enemy cannot condemn us, that's for sure. The Bible tells us that God is faithful, so we're going to hold on to that promise. There can be no condemnation then; we have to keep on believing, having faith in God, and never give up until we receive what we've believed.

If we don't get our healing on earth, we'll get it in heaven. Why? Well there is no sickness in heaven and everyone is perfect and whole in heaven with new heavenly bodies. We win, whichever way. Nevertheless, I don't know about you, but while I'm still on this earth, I'm going to fight the good fight of faith because I want my healing here on earth as well. That's why we pray; "Your will be done on earth as it is in heaven." We're going to be healed one day in heaven that's a fact, but Jesus died on the Cross so that we could be healed on earth as well. We shouldn't be giving up, and we shouldn't stop fighting just because nothing has happened or changed within our situation or need. We never know when the miracle is going to manifest and break through. We've got to be like the woman with the issue of blood for twelve years. Press on and say to yourself; "I will be healed, I'm going to be healed," and we don't give up saying it and believing it. Be like the guy next to the pool for thirty-eight years, having no chance at all of getting into the pool by himself to be healed. Nevertheless, he laid there for all those years, believing that someday something was going to happen, and maybe someone will help him into the pool so that he can be healed. That, my friend, was faith. This guys endured and just kept on believing never giving up. Let our spirit man be satisfied with what we speak and let it sustain us when we're attacked and going through a trial or tribulation. That's how we're going to get through all of these attacks coming from the enemy; when our spirit man is strong and full of God's Word, it will carry us through and help us to receive the victory.

As an example I like using is my diesel truck that I drive. It's a diesel, not a gas truck. So if I fill up my diesel truck with normal fuel, or gas, what do you think is going to happen? Well, it'll run for a few miles and then the engine will stop working. It'll break down. Why? Well, it's a diesel truck, and I put normal gas in it. I put the wrong gas into it. It was not made to run on normal gas but to run on diesel. The same applies to us, in our Christian lives. If we put negative, fear-filled, doubtful, unbelieving words into our spirit man, it'll work for a while, but eventually our spirit man will break down into a broken spirit. We'll think we're okay, but as soon as the calamity comes, our spirit man cannot and will not sustain us. We've filled our spirit man with the wrong gas, the wrong words. We're stuck, going nowhere, and we can't move forward to receive our promise and victory. That's when we start to function in hybridized faith, faith mixed with fear, unbelief and doubt and by now we all know that there will be no success by using this kind of faith.

Our spirit man should be receiving the Word of God. We are to function and live from God's Word, not the devil's lies and fear-filled words that he offers us. We have to run on God's fuel, the power of God's Word, not the devil's fuel or negative fear-filled words. We were created to put God's Word, or fuel, into our spirit man. We were created by God's Word and we should be healed by God's Words. So why are so many of us broken-down vessels? Why do we have broken spirits? Maybe we're using the wrong fuel, or putting the wrong words into our spirit man. Check yourselves, make sure you're not filling up at the wrong gas pump.

If we know that all is well in that area, that we're filling up our spirit man with the right kind words, and the attacks still keep coming, then most probably the devil's just coming around again and attacking us and trying to discourage and torment us. If it is Satan attacking us again, we have to get up, move forward and fight, never giving up until we overcome the enemy through our mustard seed faith. We are children of God, and a child of God has the Holy Spirit inside of him. We fight with the power of God's Word. We fight with the power that we have received from the Holy Spirit, and we never give up. We are victorious through Christ Jesus, always remember that. So let's move forward and get our promises that God promised us in His Word.

We have more power, and greater power, than the enemy has guys. We have the resurrection power of the Holy Spirit living inside of us. Use the power and the authority that God has given us. Then, by our faith, pure powerful mustard seed faith, let's be healed, be whole, let's be set free, be delivered, be saved, and be prosperous in all things. All things include our jobs, family, church, children. It includes prospering emotionally, spiritually, physically, and financially. Let's receive our blessings by exercising our mustard seed faith. Start living in this manner of faith and believe that it's going to work and you'll see things starting to change.

So let's sum it up like this. When we ask God in faith, to supply a specific need that we have, or to heal us, deliver us, save us, protect and prosper us, and we don't hybridize our faith with fear, doubt, or any other contaminated seed coming from the enemy, we're releasing our mustard seed faith—faith-filled words. That's when our inner man, our spirit man, will be satisfied with the fruit that comes from our mouths. It'll be satisfied with the words of life that we're speaking. That's when our spirit man helps us, sustain us, and upholds us through the attacks, the sicknesses, calamities, and the trials. That's how we receive what we have spoken. That's how we're healed by our faith.

A good example of the above is when God told Joshua to lead the Israelites into the land of Canaan. This is the first leader that God had told to lead the nation according to the Word of God that was written down. If Joshua was going to have success and be prosperous, as a leader, he was going to have to read the Word of God, speak it, and do what it said he should be doing. God knew Joshua was going to speak these words, and the words that he would speak would create an image, either of success and prosperity or of defeat.

> This Book of the Law *shall not depart from your mouth, but you shall meditate in it day and night, that you may observe to do according to all that is written in it.* For then *you will make your way prosperous, and then you will have good success.*
>
> —Joshua 1:8, emphasis mine

The bottom line is this: Joshua was going to have to get into the Word of God, the book of the Law. He was going to have to speak the Word of God and meditate in it, day and night. In other words, read it, hear it, speak it, and believe it. He was going to have to look and see what was written in it, and do what it said he should be doing. That's how he was going to have to have success and going to be prosperous in what God had told him to do. This will work for us too, guys. God is the same yesterday, today, and forever. He does not change, nor does His Word. We also have to get into the Word of God and read it, speak it day and night, and continually observe, or look, to see what it says, what is written in it, and then do what it says. That's when we'll be prosperous and have good success as well, just like Joshua had success and prospered. That's God's promise is to all of us. Take these promises, accept them, and receive them. Let's speak God's Word, and then let's do God's Word. This will create mustard seed faith in us, and give us success and prosper us. Job 22:28 says it beautifully: *"You will also declare a thing, And it will be established for you*; So light will shine on your ways." (emphasis mine). Oh my! Job is saying hey guys if you will only speak God's healing Word and declare your healing it is going to be established for you, it's going to come to pass. He says we'll have light on our way, the opposite to darkness, sickness, or any other evil attack from Satan" Isn't that great news? Now let's look at how we can practically apply our mustard seed faith in our daily lives.

CHAPTER 9

Applying Mustard Seed Faith

S ome of you might wonder how I personally apply mustard seed faith in my own life. Now you have to remember, I am just a normal guy like everyone else. I battle with this hybridized faith as well. No one said it was going to be easy to stop the contaminated seeds of fear, doubt, unbelief, anger, worry, stress, and many more from trying to hybridize with our faith. Every person is going to be attacked by these contaminated seeds, I can promise you that. But we have to spiritually fight these hybridizing attacks, and keep our faith pure like a mustard seed as much as we can. We have to do this so that we can see the power of the mustard seed faith work for us. I agree with David when he said that we have to get more serious about the power of God's Word. The power of the Word of God is what is going to produce the mustard seed faith in us, and then, this faith will bring forth success and prosperity. David said it this way:

Concerning the works of men, *By the word of Your lips, I have kept away from the paths of the destroyer.*

—Psalm 17:4, emphasis mine

David was basically saying, and I'm paraphrasing; "God, I took the words of Your mouth, from Your lips, and put them into my heart, into my spirit, and into my own mouth. I spoke these words by faith. The Word filled my spirit man and satisfied it until I saw things the way that You see them. That's why the enemy could not touch me, harm me, or destroy me, and I was healed. That's how I stayed out of the enemy's way." David basically confessed that because of the words coming from God's mouth, God's lips, he, David, was able to keep and stay out of the path of the devil, the enemy. That's success and victory right there!

That's a great truth coming from David. So how can we stay out of the path of the enemy? We get God's Word into our spirit man continually by speaking it with our mouths, that's it, no further discussion. Too many Christians are not doing this and obviously not functioning by mustard seed faith. That's why they're sinking instead of walking on top of the storm. I'm reminding you again: Hybridized faith will not work; it makes us sink into the storm, just like Peter did. Only mustard seed faith has the power to make us succeed, to make us walk on top of the storm and have victory. "So how do you use mustard seed faith Hansie," you might be asking?

The first thing that I do is this: Every time that I quote a scripture concerning faith, I make an effort to remind myself that I'm not talking about hybrid faith, but mustard seed faith. I have to remind myself as well that every time that Jesus, Paul, John, Peter, or any of the other disciples spoke about faith, that they were talking about mustard seed faith, not hybridized faith. "How can you say that, and how do you know that?" you might ask. Well, if they were not talking about mustard seed faith, but about hybridized faith, then the following scriptures could not be relevant and true. Let's look at some scriptures we've already used: Let's use the same scriptures that we quoted in the Introduction section:

1. We have to live by faith: "For in it the righteousness of God is revealed from faith to faith; as it is written, "The just shall *live by faith*," (Romans 1:17). As you can see, as righteous believers, we have to live by faith every day of our lives.

2. We have to have faith to please God: Hebrews 11:6 says, "But *without faith it is impossible to please Him*, for he who comes to God must believe that He is, and that He is a rewarder of those who diligently seek Him." When we put our faith in God that He will heal, save, deliver, and supply all our needs, that's when we please God.

3. We need faith to resist the devil: 1 Peter 5:8–9 instructs us to "Be sober, be vigilant; because your adversary the devil walks about like a roaring lion, seeking whom he may devour. *Resist him, steadfast in the faith*, knowing that the same sufferings are experienced by your brotherhood in the world." When the devil attacks us, and we're trusting God to help us and protect us, that's when we're using our faith to resist the enemy.

4. We need faith to fight the spiritual war: 1 Timothy 6:12 tells us to "*Fight the good fight of faith*, lay hold on eternal life, to which you were also called

and have confessed the good confession in the presence of many witnesses." We are not fighting a physical battle; we're fighting a spiritual fight so we must use our faith to fight with;

5. We overcome the world with our faith: 1 John 5:4 says, "For whatever is born of God overcomes the world. And *this is the victory that has overcome the world—our faith*." While we're fighting with our faith, we'll be able to overcome the world and the problems of the world.

My belief is that the faith mentioned in the above scriptures was definitely mustard seed faith and not hybridized faith that is crossbred with fear, doubt, unbelief, or with any other contaminated seed from Satan. If that's not true, then how does a Christian live by faith mixed with fear, worry, stress, doubt, unbelief, and so forth. We can't live that way. That's torment! That's opposite to the way that Jesus said we should believe. We can only live by pure mustard seed faith. How does a Christian please God with faith that's mixed with fear, doubt, and unbelief? God is not pleased when we fear, doubt, worry, stress, or have unbelief. He specifically told us in His Word to not be afraid and worry. How does a Christian resist the devil steadfast in the faith, that's mixed and hybridized with fear, doubt, unbelief, anger, and so on? We can't resist Satan with this kind of faith. The devil's the one that puts the fear, doubt, unbelief, and all the other contaminated seeds into our minds and wants to hybridize our faith with these seeds. You can't resist Satan with fear, doubt and unbelief when he's the author of it. We have to use mustard seed faith, that's what works! How do we fight the good fight of faith with hybridized faith? We can't fight with faith that is mixed with fear, doubt, anger, and unbelief. We can't fight a good fight of faith that's hybridized with these evil contaminated seeds. They're opposite to real mustard seed faith. That's totally insane and doesn't make sense. How do we overcome the world and the attacks in the world with fear, doubt, and unbelief? Fear, unbelief, doubt and so forth, are the attacks from the world. We can't fight the attacks with the attacks. I hope you're getting this? We can only achieve the victory in these scriptures when we're using mustard seed faith, not hybridized faith.

Let's not forget what we said in the previous chapters. Hybridized faith is faith that is crossbred, mixed, interbred with other contaminated seeds, and it's empowered by two power sources. It's empowered by the seed of God's Word, and secondly by the contaminated seeds from Satan. Together they create hybridized faith. In other words our faith comes from the Word of God, then it gets mixed and hybridized with fear, doubt, unbelief and other seeds that come from Satan. Our faith still exists but is weakened and nullified by the hybridized factor and does not work like it should be working. These are the two powers that create hybridized faith and like I said, it does not work. These scriptures above must be talking about mustard seed faith, which is only empowered by one source: the seed of God's Word. So, every time that I read or quote scriptures with the word *faith* in them, I make sure that I remind myself that the scriptures are talking about pure, powerful mustard seed faith that cannot be hybridized with any other seed coming from the enemy. The mustard seed faith that is so pure and powerful that it destroys all of those contaminated seeds sent by the devil.

I often keep on reminding myself of this truth. I sometimes even say; "I walk by faith, (by mustard seed faith), not by sight, or by fear, or by doubt." That's how I memorize the scriptures. Then, I personalize the scriptures. Then I verbalize them to myself because I want my spirit man to hear what I'm saying to myself, and I want my spirit man to be satisfied with what I'm saying to myself. Then when the attack comes, my spirit man is going to recall what I have spoken and will carry me through, sustain me, and help me through the trial, tribulation, and the attack. That's when I'll achieve the victory. "Give us another example of what you've just explained Hansie." Okay, let's use another faith scripture. Romans 1: 17 says that The just, or the righteous, *shall live by faith*. So when I quote this scripture it sounds like this: " I am the righteous and I am the just. I am going to live by faith today. I am going to live by mustard seed faith that is not contaminated with any fear, doubt unbelief or by any other contaminated seed from Satan. I curse and destroy the power of fear, doubt and unbelief and any other contaminated seed that wants to nullify and weaken my faith. My mustard seed faith is pure and powerful and I will live by it today. I memorize, personalize and verbalize the scripture and by doing so I hear it, believe it, and more mustard seed faith is produced. Always remember that mustard seed faith does not keep you away from attacks. Mustard seed faith helps you go through the attacks victoriously, without any fear, doubt, worry, stress, or unbelief that can stop your victory. Your faith, your mustard seed faith, will save you, heal you, deliver you, prosper you, and bring you great victories, my friends. Practice it daily and speak those scriptures into your spirit man. Don't just speak the scriptures, but believe the scriptures, and then believe that you will receive what you're saying.

I'm reminding you again that Jesus told many people that their faith had healed them. It was their faith, their mustard seed faith in God, in Jesus at that time that made them well, that healed them, and delivered them. I believe that the people who were told that their faith had healed them were people functioning by mustard seed faith, not by hybridized contaminated faith. I'm sure of that because it's the only faith that works.

So, I get up in the mornings and quote my scriptures. I speak to myself, to my body, to my finances, to all situations that I'm facing, and I do it with mustard seed faith. I rebuke and bind all fear, doubt, unbelief, anger, bitterness, discouragement and all the other contaminated seeds that I can think of before the time. Then I command healing, deliverance, prosperity, and whatever else I need, to come to pass in my body and in my life. I speak protection, health, salvation, prosperity into my own life, for my wife, for my children, my grandchildren, for our supporters, for all our family and friends. I do this every morning and every night before I go to bed. "Are you serious, Hansie, that must take a lot of time?" Yes I'm serious and yes it does take a bit of time, but not too much time. Nevertheless, what a blessing it is to see what the results are. That's how I use my mustard seed faith every day, and it works. I'd rather spend time speaking these words of life into my spirit man, instead of watching and listening to the evil wicked junk and nonsense on the television!

"Can we all be doing what you're doing Hansie, and should we all be doing it?" you may ask. Of course, everybody can be doing it. Unfortunately I cannot tell you that you should be doing it. I can only tell you that it works when you start doing it and I suggest and really think that more people should be doing it. It's every-one's own choice if they want to do it or not. It takes discipline to do it but you quickly work out when and how to do it. Every person must work out their own salvation with the Lord. That's how we grow and move forward in our Christian lives. It's better than accepting defeat, sickness, and poverty and speaking death. You and I have the same authority and power that Jesus had. We have the same Holy Spirit that Jesus had. Jesus used His authority and power when He spoke, rebuked, and commanded situations to change with the authority and the power of the Holy Spirit. Dead people, sick people, blind men, crippled people, demons, and even trees all listened to Him. Why? Because even Jesus functioned with mustard seed faith by speaking to situations and they changed. He had no fear, doubt, unbelief, worry, or stress when He cast out demons, when He healed the sick, spoke to a dead Lazarus to come alive, calmed the storms, and spoke to a sycamore tree to wither up. Jesus functioned by pure, powerful mustard seed faith that He had in His Father. So can we do it too? You bet we can, and I know God wants us to function in the same manner of faith that Jesus did. When Jesus was on His way to ascend to heaven, remember the last words He spoke to His disciples on earth?:

> "Most assuredly, I say to you, *he who believes in Me, the works that I do he will do also; and greater works than these he will do*, because I go to My Father. And *whatever you ask in My name, that I will do*, that the Father may

be glorified in the Son. *If you ask anything in My name, I will do it.*

—John 14:12–14, emphasis mine

So Jesus said to them again, "Peace to you! *As the Father has sent Me, I also send you.*"

—John 20:2, emphasis mine

As we listen to Jesus speak in the above scriptures, it clearly shows us that He was telling His disciples and us, because we are His disciples too, that God had sent Him to do a certain work on earth. Then He told the disciples, and us, to go do what He had done. How? Well, if we believe in Him and the works that He did, Jesus said that we could do the same works and even do greater works than He did. The catch is, we'll have to function with the same mustard seed faith with which Jesus had functioned. We have the same power that Jesus had because God gave us the same Holy Spirit that He had. So let's use the same mustard seed faith that Jesus used as well.

And I will pray the Father, *and He will give you another Helper, that He may abide with you forever—the Spirit of truth, whom the world cannot receive,* because it neither sees Him nor knows Him; but you know Him, for He dwells with you and will be in you. I will not leave you orphans; I will come to you.

—John 14:16–18, emphasis mine

But you shall receive power when the Holy Spirit has come upon you; and you shall be witnesses to Me in Jerusalem, and in all Judea and Samaria, and to the end of the earth."

—Acts 1:8, emphasis mine

As you can see, God gave us the same Holy Spirit that Jesus had so that we would be able to do exactly what He did. We need that same authority and power of the Holy Spirit that Jesus had, and we need that same mustard seed faith that Jesus had as well to be able to do what He did.

I don't know about you, but I want to be like Jesus. I want to follow His example and follow in His footsteps. I want to function with the same power that Jesus functioned. I want the same faith in God that Jesus had. I want to do what Jesus did and speak like Jesus did. I want my mustard seed faith to be so powerful and so pure that I can be healed, be set free, delivered, and become prosperous because of my faith. I want to pray for people with the same Holy Spirit power and anointing and use the same power of the mustard seed faith that Jesus used and see people get healed, saved and be delivered. How about you? Can we follow the example of Jesus. Of course we can. 1 Peter 2: 21-23 says; "For to this you were called, for Christ also suffered for us, *leaving us an example, that you should follow His steps.* Who committed no sin, Nor was deceit found in His mouth." (emphasis mine). The example is set, so I want to be like Jesus, and do what He did. How about you?

Now always remember that our faith, our mustard seed faith, has got to be in God. We have to have faith in God, not in money, not in people, not in things, not in doctors, lawyers, evangelists, not in the government, not in anything else or in anyone else but in God alone. The next chapter is an example of how I applied my personal mustard seed faith in a situation that Jeanette and I went through a while ago.

CHAPTER 10

Jeanette's Testimony

When my wife Jeanette got sick and the doctors gave her two percent chance to live, my faith was tested in a way that I'd never dreamed of. I will never forget how I drove her to the ER speeding down the Highway. We got to the hospital and after hearing the doctors report of how serious she was and that she needed surgery, I was immediately confronted with the spirit of fear. The doctor told me that the CT scans showed that nothing was wrong but that he still needed to operate on her. I remember telling the doctor that how could he operate if he did not know what was wrong with her. He told me that he realized I was a preacher but that he was a Christian as well, and he felt that he had to do what the Holy Spirit was telling him to do to save her life. He had to operate, or she was going to die. He just needed my permission. When I heard those words it was like mana from heaven. God had sent us a Christian doctor. What an awesome God we serve. I could only praise God and agreed for the surgery.

Thank God for Christian doctors. Now listen, that got my attention and I had no choice but to agree for the surgery to take place, immediately. Nevertheless, my faith was not in the doctor; even if he was a Christian, it was in God. I trusted God that He would lead and help the doctor and give him wisdom. I believed that God would use the expertise of the doctor so that he could perform a successful surgery and save Jeanette's life. So they took Jeanette into surgery while my pastor friends and I started praying while waiting in the waiting room. They were busy with the surgery when something unbelievable happened. The doctor called me on his cell phone while he was busy with the surgery. I've never heard of any doctor do that before. He called me to tell me what was wrong with Jeanette; she was full of poison. Two feet of her intestines had rotted and had burst open when they opened her up. Poison was everywhere, and they had a problem. The doctor called me and asked me to contact the churches that I knew, and other Christians so that they could start praying for Jeanette, and for him. Man, that was unreal—a doctor asking for prayer during a surgery.

I was still okay until the doctor told me that he had told the assistant doctor helping him, that it did not look like Jeanette was not going to make it. Then he told me, that he did not think that she was going to live and make it through the surgery. That's why he needed a lot of prayer. All the fear, stress, and worry available from the enemy came down on me. What did I do? Well, I had two choices. I could focus on what the enemy was preparing to do, trying to kill my wife, and by doing so hybridize my faith. Or, I could look at God's Word, and see what Jesus had already done for us on the cross, and by doing so keep my faith pure and powerful, and thus function with mustard seed faith. I chose the latter and started speaking life, speaking scriptures. I started proclaiming that Jeanette was not going to die, but live and declare the works of the Lord. I started rebuking and cursing fear, doubt, unbelief. I rebuked the spirit of death and infirmity. I started putting my mustard seed faith to work, refusing to hybridize my faith with Satan's contaminated seeds in spite of the hybridizing attacks and all the evidence of failure. Was it easy? Oh my goodness no, it was very hard not to look at the evidence of death hovering over Jeanette's life. I'm telling you when you come face to face with the spirit of death, it's very hard not to let your faith crumble and hybridize. Some of you know what I'm talking about. That's when I called Elize our daughter and asked her to help me get the message out to all our friends. Elize quickly put out the prayer request on Facebook for all to read that Jeanette needed prayer because she was most probably not going to make it according to statistics and the doctor. The doctor told me that only two percent of people survive this kind of surgery. The doctor was not negative; he was just giving me the facts. Those were the facts, yes, but I also knew that the truth; God's Word, could nullify a fact immediately. I had hope, and a promise from God's Word, and boy did I hold on to it.

Well, all our friends and all the churches where we minister started praying and supporting me. Where was my faith? Once again, it was not in the people but in God. I had to put my faith in God only. I believed that God was going to use the doctor and nurses and that he would hear all the supporting and uplifting prayers coming from all the people and churches around America that knew about the attack.

The doctor did what he could and with God's help he pulled her through the surgery. Then he told me that all we could do was watch and wait, and believe that

God would keep her alive. The doctor had done all that he could have done. Now it was in God's hands. I'm telling you; what a faith test I was going through. I preach and tell people how to function in situations like this, but when it comes your way, and you have to practice what you preach, it is a different story and very difficult. I'm admitting this because I want to be transparent with all of you. We preachers find it difficult to fight battles as well. We also need help and prayers, just like you all need help and prayers. Nevertheless, we can't give up, we have to keep on going forward towards the victory and the promises in God's Word. If I had not had mustard seed faith, I don't think I would have made it. I would have started fearing, doubting, having unbelief, and speaking death. All odds were against Jeanette, and I could easily have hybridized my faith with those contaminating seeds from Satan. I can assure you that we could have ended up having a bad tragedy and the situation could of ended up looking much differently than it did end up in being.

I remember thinking, "what am I supposed to do now?" Then I realized that I was already functioning in mustard seed faith because I found myself speaking the Word of God out of my mouth, like a recorded message, repeating the scriptures over and over. It just didn't stop. It just kept on coming out of my mouth all the time, automiatically. I was quoting scripture after scripture. It was like my spirit man was refusing to give in to the circumstances around me. My spirit man was actually refusing to accept that my wife was going to die. I realized that my spirit man was feeding me all the scriptures that I had spoken into it for all these years. I was busy withdrawing from my spiritual bank account. My spirit man was busy sustaining me, helping me, uplifting me and carrying me through this attack and devastating situation. I still remember that I asked God why I was able to be so calm yet so concerned. I wondered where all the people came from that called me on my cell, and where all these people came from that were supporting Jeanette and me in this incredibly difficult death situation. Within five minutes after we put it out on Facebook, I got calls, text messages, and emails from hundreds of people, uplifting us and speaking scriptures into our lives. Dear pastor friends of ours and their wives, were there in the hospital lifting me up, praying with me, for me and for Jeanette. I'm telling you, that really lifted up my faith. I was hearing myself and others speaking life into my spirit man, confirming that Jeanette was going to live and not die. The Word of God that I was hearing was producing more and more mustard seed faith and causing me to have absolutely no fear, no doubt, and no unbelief. Oh yes, the contaminated seeds tried to break through and hybridize with my faith, that's a fact. Nevertheless, my mustard seed faith in God was busy destroying these seeds of fear, doubt, unbelief and discouragement one by one.

"So why were you so calm, Hansie?" When I asked God about it, He was quick to remind me of my spiritual bank account that was filled with the Word of God. God reminded me of all the scriptures I had spoken into my spirit man. It was now playing back to me, and my spirit man was busy sustaining me, helping me, holding me up, and carrying me through this situation because of the Word that was deposited into it. I was withdrawing from my spiritual bank account where I had deposited many scriptures over many years. Then God reminded me of how many people I had prayed for, for healing, for salvation and for other issues in revival services. He reminded me of how many people I had prayed for at three o'clock in the morning when everyone else was sleeping. He reminded me of how many times I had given and shown love and compassion and prayed for others, everywhere at any time. He told me that I had sown so much into other people's lives, that I had sown time, love, concern, prayers of healing, encouragement, and so forth. Now it was time to harvest what I had sown into people's lives for almost twenty years that we've been ministering in America. I was reaping what I had sown into people's lives. I was busy withdrawing from my spiritual bank account. What a reward I was receiving, and I needed it so desperately. So let me ask you today: how full is your spiritual bank account? Can you withdraw if you have to, or are you on a zero balance? It might be a good time to check your spiritual bank account balance. You might need to withdraw someday.

Again, all of this was not easy. Many times I was reminded by the devil that my wife was going to die and could die. Every time that I heard that voice, I had to shake my head and say: "Nope, that would be the day Satan in Jesus name. Oh no, she's not going to die; she will live and declare the works of the Lord." You see, I know that Satan comes to steal, kill, and destroy, but Jesus came to give us life. So I kept on proclaiming life, and kept on speaking it to myself and to Jeanette as she laid there in ICU in a coma, not waking up like the doctors wanted her to. While all of this was taking place, my spirit man was at work, busy sustaining me all the time, lifting me up, helping me, and encouraging me through this situation with the word of God, that I had spoken and written into it with my tongue.

After a few days they had taken Jeanette off of all the meds that they had her on during the surgery, so that she could wake up, but she did not wake up. There was no reaction from her side. That was not a good sign according to the doctor and we had a problem! For a whole ten days she didn't wake up, and for the whole ten days the devil told me to wake up and see that the end was near. It got really bad when two people on either side of Jeanette's room in ICU died following a similar surgery. The one died on the Monday and the other on the Tuesday. That was the enemy's biggest trial and attack of fear and doubt that he had put in front of my eyes to see. The enemy quickly let me know that Jeanette was next in line to die. Oh my goodness, that made me go down to the hospital restaurant downstairs and have a serious talk to God. I could have given up right there, I was so discouraged at that point, but I chose to talk to God, to ask Him to help me and show me what to do. Those contaminated seeds from Satan were doing all they could to hybridize with my faith and get me to give up and let go of God's promise, but I held on to God. Discouragement was the worst seed attacking me at that point of time.

The doctors wanted to take out the ventilator, but Jeanette was not reacting, so they couldn't. The reason was that if they had taken out the ventilator and her breathing was not strong enough, then she could have stopped breathing and she most probably would have died. That's what the doctor was telling us. I also remembered that Jeanette had told me not to let her live if a machine was keeping her alive. So the question was this; should I tell them to take out the ventilator or not? I had to take the risk and make the choice, hoping that she would breathe on her own and live, or not breath, and die. That was a very hard decision to make. So I had a talk with God. I told God that I promise Him, that if it was Jeanette's time to die, it would be okay. I told Him that I would release her that same day if it was her time to die and go home. I did not want her to die, but I was okay with it if it was her time to go. That was an even harder decision to make to release her, but it took a lot of pressure off of me. That's when my mustard seed faith in God started to rise up in power again. Then I told God that I did not know if it was her time to die and go to heaven, so I was not going to accept that it was her time to die. God had not told me that it was her time to die. Oh the devil had whispered that into my ears, yes, but not God. I knew that we all had a time to die, and that was okay with me, but how did I know if it was Jeanette's time to die? So I told God I was going to fight until she blew out her last breath. Until then, my faith was not going to waver or give in, or stop functioning or be hybridized. I was not going to let Satan's lies consume me and his seeds contaminate and hybridize with my faith. I was going to keep my faith pure, powerful, and alive. I was going to keep on living by faith and functioning by mustard seed faith. And I did! That's what got me through the attack, my mustard seed faith in God.

I promised God that I would keep on serving Him and keep on ministering whatever happened. So the Lord spoke to me and said: "Go tell the doctor to take out the ventilator and Jeanette would wake up within ten minutes." I immediately went up to the room in ICU, and with all the mustard seed inside of me I gave them the order, and the doctor came and took out the ventilator. I still remember my daughter Lizelle, asking me if I was sure that it was the right decision that I was making. I told her what God had told me to do, and we both just agreed and asked God to do the miraculous miracle that only He could do. Did Jeanette wake up? Nope! She was still in a coma but at least she was alive, she was breathing praise the Lord. Listen, at that moment I almost gave in to discouragement and doubt again, right there. You see Satan never gives up trying to hybridize our faith. God immediately reminded me that He had said ten minutes and then she'd wake up. It was only at about the five or six minutes mark at that point of time. I give God all the praise because at about the eight minute mark she started opening those green eyes very slowly. Within ten minutes, just as God had told me, she started talking and asking for water. My friends, you could not believe my praise and thankfulness toward God for His unmeasurable love and faithfulness at that point of time. She woke up completely from the coma and after a few hours they took her to a normal room — no more ICU. She was awake and alive. Praise be to our God, and thank You Lord Jesus for Your blood and the stripes that healed Jeanette. Thank You Lord for Your faithfulness.

I want to give God all the praise and glory for this miracle, but I also want to thank all of our friends, pastors and churches that prayed with us, supported us financially, and lifted us up in this time of tribulation. What great power there is when believers stand together in agreement and pray. Our God is an awesome God and we have great friends and churches all over America. Jeanette was in the hospital for forty days in total. We had to keep on fighting infection because they were still trying to get rid of all the poison that could still kill her. Every day the doctor came to see her, he just kept shaking his head. He just kept on saying that God surely had done a miracle. He told Jeanette every day that she should have been dead, but that God had saved and healed her. She was a walking miracle. Nevertheless, being in hospital for so long caused her little body to become very weak and she received many days of rehab to learn to walk again and do normal tasks. It was a slow recovery process. The miracle of staying life had taken place, and now the healing had to take place. We are still going through some issues and we're still fighting the good fight of faith believing God for her complete healing at this point in time.

Nevertheless, can you imagine what could have happened if all our friends around the country, all the churches and even myself, if we had not used our mustard seed faith, but instead had used hybridized faith? What a disaster that could have been! We all most probably would have given up and spoken words of death, or fear-filled words and negative words. Would Jeanette have died if we had used hybridized faith, or would she have lived? Who knows? I don't know, but what I do know is this: if she had died while we were functioning in hybridized faith, the enemy would have come in with a knockout blow. He would have condemned all of us, especially me, with words like: "You did not pray hard enough. You did not speak the Word enough. Your faith never worked. You never had enough faith to believe that your wife was going to live. You're a man of fear, not of faith and so are all of your friends. You're the reason why she died, you're a weak Christian. Nobody will ever get healed again when you pray for them," and so forth, and so forth. Oh, he would have made me and all of us feel so guilty; that's a fact. He's doing this every day, to many believers, because they're functioning in hybridized faith and not with mustard seed faith. Satan is condemning them because family or friends have died, or never got healed, and some believers struggle with guilt for years thereafter. They believe it's their fault. What a lie from the devil once again.

I don't know if you agree with me, but all I know is that if I speak life, like we all did with Jeanette's story, and we speak God's Word, we give ourselves, and our loved ones, a chance to receive healing and victory. If we don't, and we speak death and hybridize our faith, we don't give ourselves, or our family any chance of victory or success. So I'd rather fight the good fight of faith, with mustard seed faith, and let God do what He does best. He's our Healer, our Comforter, our Savior, and our Deliverer. God is our Father and He will supply all our needs according to His riches in glory by Christ Jesus is what Philippians 4:19 says. All that we have to do is to apply and use our mustard seed faith that we have in God. That's when we'll have good success, and that's when we can expect to prosper in all things and see results and miracles.

I want to encourage you all to start exercising mustard seed faith. When things go wrong and the attacks come, stand up, pull back your shoulders, and proclaim that you are a child of God. Open your mouth, and speak the Word of God. Make sure that you speak life, not death. Make sure that you never give up until the victory comes. But what if you're doing all of the above and your wife or love one still dies, and they still do not get healed? Maybe your son is still hooked on drugs and dies of an overdose or goes to prison in any case? What do you do when nothing changes but even gets worse?

All I can say is this: When we function with mustard seed faith, at least we're not giving up in the fighting process, and we're doing all that we could be doing.

That's better than functioning in hybridized faith that does not work at all. One thing I learned from Jeanette being so close to death is that you never, never ever give up. You fight the good fight of faith until it's over and you get the victory. Remember what I told God: that I would keep on fighting until she blew out her last breath. I would not give up believing, speaking life, and fighting with my mustard seed faith. If your loved ones do not get healed on earth, it's sad when they die and go home, I realize that. I can only imagine what it feels like. I can identify a little bit with those people who have lost loved ones because it was a close call with Jeanette. Nevertheless, they will still get their healing in heaven because there is no sickness in heaven. They're going to have a new heavenly body, healed in perfection. So whatever happens, they win, and we win, knowing that they are home and healed united with God the Father.

Many people ask me if I think that their faith had not worked because their loved one died in spite of all the prayers. My own personal thought on this is, no, I know and believe that your faith did work. Some have asked but why did God not heal the sick person on earth? We will never know that answer; someday in heaven we'll know why. I see it this way; if it is someone's time to die and go home, they'll go. If God does not give them extra time like He did with Hezekiah, they're gone. That's how it works. The Bible says that there's a time to be born and *a time to die*; Ecclesiastes 3: 2. Then I realized something else while Jeanette was in hospital. This might help some people.

When she woke up after being in the coma, she told me about two incidents, dreams, visions, or maybe real life situations that she had, we don't really know for sure what had happened to her. She said in the first incident or dream she had, she found herself on a train station. There was a train, and many people were getting onto the train. She tried to talk to these people to find out where they were going. They did not acknowledge her presence at all. They did not even look at her, could not see her, and did not talk to her, they just kept boarding the train. It was like they could not acknowledge that she was there. Then all of a sudden the train conductor was standing in front of her. She told me that it was the most gorgeous-looking man with the bluest eyes she's ever seen. He had this peace on his face. He did not speak to her with his mouth but through his eyes. He asked her if she was ready to come and join them and go with them. She answered him with her eyes as well, and told him that she wanted to stay with her husband and wanted to be at her daughter's wedding. He just smiled at her and then left and disappeared.

The second experience that she had was where multitudes of people were boarding a big cruise ship. Same thing happened again. She tried talking to the people asking them where they were going, but no one responded and even acknowledged her being there. When she looked up the same man with the same blue eyes and smile was there. This time he was dressed as the ship's captain. He came to her with those blue eyes piercing into her with love and kindness, full of gentleness and peace. Again he spoke to her with his eyes and asked her if she was ready to go with them this time. Once again she answered him with her own eyes that he must forgive her, but she was going to stay. She wanted to see her daughter Elize get married, and she wanted to stay with me, her husband. He just smiled again and spoke with his eyes, "It's okay, he said," left and disappeared.

These two incidents got my attention, and I wondered who she had talked to? Was it Jesus? Was it an angel? Who knows? It definitely was not Satan that came with a peace and love attitude, that's for sure! You can see that I spelled the "he" with lower case letters in the above sentences because we don't exactly know who it was that spoke to her. Nevertheless, if it was Jesus or an angel, had God given Jeanette a choice, to choose if she wanted to go to heaven or to stay? We don't know. In both those incidents, were all those people boarding the train and ship on their way to heaven? Who knows? Why could she not talk to them and why did they not acknowledge her being there? All I know is that she said it was so peaceful. There was no fear or sadness, only love. Now I want you to listen to the following very carefully and don't shoot me down. This is my own opinion. Let's assume that it was Jeanette's time to die and go home, but God had given her a choice to come home, or to stay on earth. She obviously had made the choice to stay, right, because she's alive today? What if she had chosen not to stay, but to go, and had died and gone to heaven because it was her time to go any case? Would my faith have failed and not worked? What about all the people that had prayed for her? Would their faith have failed and not worked? Oh no, I don't believe that. You see, we all used our mustard seed faith to the full. We all spoke life and declared healing over Jeanette, even when we couldn't see it. That was mustard seed faith that we exercised in fullness. If it was her time to die go home, then we had not wasted our time praying and believing, and it's not that our faith had not worked. No, we had fought the good fight of faith, and we had done what God had expected us to do. If it was her time to go and she had chosen to go as her life had been

116

planned by God, we did not lose at all, and our faith was not in vain, oh no! She would have gone to heaven and received her healing in any case where there is no sickness or death. Man this opened my eyes to some things I had battled with. Look at the next point. Secondly, let's accept that it was not her time to die go home, but God still gave her a choice to stay, or to go to heaven. Let's say she said yes, and she chose to die and go to heaven, choosing to go with the cruise ship, or even on the train! How would any of us have known that God had given her a choice? Many of us would have thought that our faith had not worked. In the meantime it was not the case of our faith not working, no, it was Jeanette that had chosen to go home even if it was not her time yet. Oh my goodness, this changed everything for me. So I figured it out like this!

When somebody dies, then we have to accept that it could be their time to go. On the other hand we must also consider the fact that maybe they chose to go, because they were given a choice to stay or go to heaven. God could've have given them a choice. Who knows? How could we know, or would we have known what had expired between the sick person and God? We would never know if God had given them a choice, or not. Maybe they saw those blue eyes and the love in them and decided that earth was not the place for them anymore. It doesn't mean that our faith had not worked.

If Jeanette had decided to go and it wasn't her time, were all our prayers and faith in vain? No, no, not at all. We would never have known that God had given her that choice because she would be dead, and she would never have been able to tell me about the choices, right? I'm repeating this again because it's important. We did what God's Word told us to do. We did our part as believers; that's for sure. The praying and believing made us get into the Word of God. The Word of God built our faith and strengthened our faith even more. It made us more mature in Christ, and it gave us more endurance and strength. That's how you and I can keep on fighting like good strong soldiers of Jesus Christ. We never stop believing and applying our mustard seed faith, and we never ever give up, it doesn't matter what happens or whichever way it goes. We hold on to Jesus. I'm glad that Jeanette chose to stay of course, because I did not want to lose my wife. We'll never know if it was her time to go and if God gave her a choice; or if it was not her time to go and God still gave her a choice to go to heaven or stay with her husband. The fact of the matter is she's alive and well, praise God! But remember this point in the future when someone dies and you've prayed and believed that God would heal them, and they still die. You don't know what expired between that person and God. We have to accept that fact!

That's how I used my mustard seed faith practically. It was hard, but I learned many things going through this attack. I want to urge you to do the same if you have not yet done so. Hold on to Jesus, and keep your eyes on the one who loves and cares for you. Hebrews 12:2 says, *"Looking unto Jesus, the author and finisher of our faith, who for the joy that was set before Him endured the cross*, despising the shame, and has sat down at the right hand of the throne of God" (emphasis mine).

Let our mustard seed faith take us through every attack, trial, calamity, and tribulation. If we don't give up and we keep on fighting, we'll see how faithful God is. That's when the victories, salvations, healings, deliverance and successes will come. That's how you and I resist Satan, overcome the world, and become victorious, by being steadfast in our faith, in our mustard seed faith. "Hansie, do you ever think that maybe God sent this sickness so that you and Jeanette could get more faith, and become stronger Christians," someone asked me the other day? Are you kidding me? Absolutely not! There is no way that God put Jeanette in hospital where she almost died so that we could get more faith. I definitely don't believe that at all. Faith does not come through God letting your intestines burst open and poison filling your body so that you almost die. Faith does not come by God giving you cancer or letting you get sick unto death. The Bible does not have such a verse in the scripture, nowhere. The Bible says that faith comes by hearing, hearing the Word of God, Romans 10:17 says. My faith grew because when Jeanette got sick, guess what I did? I got into the Word of God and applied the Word to her situation. The Word of God produced faith, mustard seed faith, in me and in all of us and we believed that God would heal her, and He did. For the interest sake, Hebrews 11: 6 says that God is a rewarder of those who diligently seek Him. God does not make people sick, cause divorces, or steals money. He is *a rewarder of those of us who diligently seek Him.* If I remember correctly, Satan comes to steal kill and to destroy, Jesus came to give us life. God and Satan has never changed places. Satan is the still stealer, and God is still the Healer. Nothing's changed! I can definitely tell you that I know that the devil put my wife in hospital to kill her, not God. God heard and answered our prayers and sent His Word and healed her. God does not hurt us and make us sick and then comes and heals us afterwards, oh no, I don't believe that at all. It's like you and I putting our child's hand on a hot stove and

119

burning it because they were disobedient. Then saying oh I'm sorry and then putting medicine on the burn to heal it. What kind of parent does such a wicked deed. Same scenario. God does not do such wicked deeds, He's a good Father, He's a healer, not a destroyer. That's the truth right there and that's how I believe! If other people believe differently, they are welcome to do so. We all have our own opinions, right? Thank You Jesus that You still perform miracles and I praise You that You are a healer and not a stealer! According to our faith, our mustard seed faith, we can be healed and Jeanette was healed.

Conclusion

S o, how do I conclude the power of the mustard seed faith? We can talk about faith forever; it's an ongoing power that we have received from God and a never-ending subject. As believers, we have to live by mustard seed faith every single day of our lives. We have to have mustard seed faith in God and in no one else, and in nothing else. We have to keep our mustard seed faith pure and clean from any other contaminated seeds and influences from the outside. We have to make sure that no fear, no doubt, no unbelief, no worry, stress, or any other contaminated seed from the devil can crossbreed and hybridize with our faith. The way that we do that is by speaking God's Word which will create mustard seed faith in us, then the mustard seed faith will destroy the seeds of fear, doubt, unbelief and any other contaminated seed sent by Satan.

We have to speak life, Gods Word—nothing else. We have to refuse to speak the sickness, the problem, or the attack. We rather have to speak life, the answer, the victory, over and over until our faith- filled words destroys all the fear, doubt, unbelief, and other seeds sent by Satan. We must never give up, and we must never let hybridizing take place in our faith life. We must realize that we are overcomers by the blood of the Lamb and by the words that we speak—never forget that.

> *And they overcame him by the blood of the Lamb and by the word of their testimony*, and they did not love their lives to the death.

> —Revelation 12:11, emphasis mine

In conclusion I want to answer a question that I could have answered in the beginning of the book but left it until now on purpose. The measure of faith that God has given to every person on earth according to Romans 12:2, what kind of faith was that? What kind of faith does God give to every person? Does He give us hybridized faith, or mustard seed faith? I can say this in boldness. I definitely know that God gave us all a measure of mustard seed faith. God won't give us a measure of faith that is already hybridized with fear, worry, doubt, stress, and unbelief. From day one our faith has always been pure and powerful. It has always had the power to remove mountains and to destroy any contaminated seed coming from Satan.

The devil has always known that we have this faith power, and he's always known that if we used it against him, we would have enormous victories over his attacks. So what did he do? He infiltrated our minds and slowly started deceiving us. He started with Adam and Eve, remember? He made them think that God was withholding a blessing from them by not wanting them to eat from the tree in the middle of the garden. The devil eventually got it right to deceive mankind, and he started it with his hybridizing tactics. Man slowly allowed the contaminated seeds of fear, doubt, unbelief, worry, stress, and many more to mix, crossbreed and hybridize with their mustard seed faith and contaminate it. Adam and Eve's faith was hybridized with disobedience and doubt about what God had told them to do. Unfortunately it did not stop with Adam and Eve and since then, all of mankind has never stopped hybridizing their faith because Satan has never stopped his hybridizing attacks.

Today Christians are doing exactly what Adam and Eve had started doing. We've started fearing, doubting, having unbelief when attacks come, and we've been living disobedient lives and we've been speaking those hybridized negative words through our mouths. We've started speaking death and claiming death into our situations. We've started calling things dead, which are not dead yet, instead of calling things that are dead, as if though they are alive. Did you get that? Read it again! We've allowed fear, doubt, and unbelief to infiltrate our faith and hybridize with it. Let me explain it with some examples. Some of us have spoken death into our finances and into our bodies before it was even there. "Yes, but it looked like it was going to go that way, Hansie," you might say. Yes you're right, it did look that way, but by speaking death, instead of life, into situations before they are dead, that's when we're giving God no chance at all to show us His power? Then, we obviously don't see miracles and healings and that's when we experience almost zero results. We get discouraged, we start functioning and living by hybridized faith, and as all of you should know by now; this kind of faith does not work.

We all know that God can do anything because nothing is impossible for God, but we still choose to speak fear and doubt-filled words and for some or other reason, we cannot believe that God is going to perform His promises. Many people call themselves sick before they are sick: "I'm just so sick and tired of this marriage and these children of mine. I'm so sick and tired of my job and my life. I get the flu every year, usually in February." Then we wonder why we're always tired and always getting sick and why our bodies are falling apart. We'll have to look at this very seriously and change our vocabulary and our way of speaking. That's how we call things dead that are not yet dead. We're not sick yet, but we're calling it as if though it is.

I believe there are people that have spoken themselves into their graves and have died before it was their time to go to heaven. I honestly think they could still be alive. How can I make such a statement? Well, if we keep on speaking death and sickness over ourselves, the possibility is there, that we might start believing that we're going to be sick and even die. We even start believing that God does not want to heal us and that He's not going to heal us. People give up on life; their spirit man becomes broken and does not sustain them. We actually call calamities that are not, as if though they are, and that's not good guys. It's time to reverse those negative destructing words. Let's go back to the tombs which we ourselves have created, there where all our dead situations are buried. It's time to roll away those stones and command those dead situations to come alive, just like Jesus did with Lazarus. We can do the same and raise up all the Lazarus's that we've created in our own lives, and of course raise the dead situations that Satan has created too. We can command these dead situations to be resurrected through our mustard seed faith. How do we do that? We speak life into those dead situations with the authority and power of the Holy Spirit by using the Word of God. Hey, most of these dead situations were created by us because we spoke them into existence, so we have to raise them from the dead! It's our own responsibility. Command them to be raised from the dead and to live!

Sometimes we almost sound like the Israelites after God had brought them out of the land of Egypt. They were blessed when He opened the Red Sea for them. He gave them water, manna, and meat, and none of them were sick or feeble. Their shoes did not even wear out. After all these miracles and after God had helped them through the desert, they listened to the ten spies complaining about the giants and the big cities in Canaan, instead of listening and remembering God's promises. So what did they do? They heard about the giants and fortified cities from these ten spies, and they couldn't believe that God could take care of those problems, so they feared, doubted and got discouraged. They hybridized their faith with these contaminated seeds and walked in unbelief. Guess what happened next? They did not enter the land of rest, the land of Canaan that God had promised them. They actually spoke themselves out of Canaan, the Promised Land. They said to each other in Numbers 14:2, "We should rather go back to Egypt or *die in the desert.*" That's when God got fed up with them and told Moses in Numbers 14:28, to tell them that *just as they had spoken in His hearing, it would be done to them.* You see they spoke hybridized faith words and spoke death over themselves before it was there. They spoke things that were alive, as if though they were dead. God said He'd take care of the giants and the cities in Canaan, but they said that God hated them and wanted to kill them and their families. How ridiculous! Faith mixed with disobedience, complaining, fear, unbelief, stress and words of death caused them to fail. (You can read that whole story in Deuteronomy 1:19-36). So what happened? They lost their promise. They walked around in the desert for forty years, and all of them died there. Just as they had believed, and just as they had spoken, that's the way it happened. Their children, twenty years old and younger, as well as Joshua and Caleb were the only ones to enter the Promised Land. Talk about a tragedy brought upon yourself through your own words. Do you realize that these Israelites changed their own destiny; they changed their whole future. They actually changed history. God wanted them in Canaan, but they changed everything because they had spoken hybridized faith-words, words of death. They believed these words and called those things that were alive as if though they were dead. Their situation ended up being dead because they never received their promise they died in the desert. The Bible should have had scriptures in it mentioning how all of the Israelites had entered into the promised land of Canaan, and how that God had taken care of the giants and fortified cities just like He took care of the Red Sea and the Egyptians. But no, it tells us that they did not get to the Promised land, they died in the desert just as they had spoken. They spoke that, what was not there, into existence. They were not going to die in the land of Canaan, God never said that! God was taking them into victory. They decided that they should rather die in the desert. They decided that God could not take care of the giants and big cities in Canaan. They spoke it and it happened. This was so sad. Watch out that we don't change our future and rewrite our own history because of what we speak guys, it's not worth it. Don't do what the Israelites did! Watch your words and your speech!

Don't forget that every seed that the devil sends is contaminated, and it's going to try to hybridize with our faith. It will destroy and weaken our faith if we allow it too. If we don't allow it, then our mustard seed faith will destroy and nullify all the seeds of fear, doubt, unbelief, worry, stress, discouragement and many more. Mustard seed faith works, and it will give you and I the victory and the success that God's Word has promised us.

To summarize everything. How does our faith heal us, or make us whole? How does our faith prosper us? If Jesus was on earth today would He be able to say to you and me, "Your faith has healed you. Your faith has made you well. Go; be made whole according to what you believe. You are healed because of your faith." The only way that that can work is when we get the Word of God into our mouths and speak it. Our ears hear it. That Word goes into our spirit man. Our spirit man then digests the Word of God and creates pure mustard seed faith in us. Then when we're faced with a challenge, sickness, a trial or an attack, we'll have to release the mustard seed faith that was formed through the Word of God in our spirit man. How do we release it? We release the pure, powerful mustard seed faith-filled words through our mouths. Our ears hear it again, and the words will go back into our spirit man. More stronger and powerful mustard seed faith will be formed. We speak it again and again, and pure mustard seed faith-filled words come out of our mouths, again and again. That's how we speak healing, wholeness, prosperity, deliverance, and salvation over ourselves and over our loved ones and into our lives. It works, because God's Word is the power of God that was sent to heals us.

Remember that God created us through His Word, so He can heal us through His Word, and He wants to heal us through His Word.

I'm going to say this one more time; the more you speak God's Word, the more you hear God's Word. The more you hear God's Word, the more you believe God's Word. We have nothing to lose by doing this. This is what Jesus meant when He said that if we speak to the mountain, and we command it to be removed and be cast into the sea, and we do not doubt, (hybridize our faith), but believe (have faith) in our hearts (our spirit man), that what we say (speak) will come to pass. That's when *we will have what we have said*. That's how mustard seed faith works!

The other side of the equation is that we don't speak life, like I've explained in the previous chapters, but then we have to face the consequences. We can go ahead and accept the sickness, the poverty, the divorce, addiction, and all the attacks from Satan, and see them as being normal life activities, and being part of our daily Christian lives. Unfortunately, when we accept this lie, we've just given ourselves absolutely no chance at all of ever getting a victory, a healing, or a miracle of any kind. That's my own personal opinion. I'd rather focus on what I can do through Christ Jesus, than focus on the problem, the attack or the destruction that's coming from Satan. I would rather speak about what Jesus has done for me on the cross, than speak about what Satan's trying to do to destroy me on earth. Satan wants to kill, steal and destroy our lives. (John 10:10). Fortunately, Jesus said that He came to give us life, in Him. Life is healing, salvation, deliverance and freedom through Christ Jesus. Thank You God for Your Son Jesus who gives us life. Let's grab hold of the life that Jesus gives and let's live in victory through our mustard seed faith.

Once again, let me give another example of how I quote scripture every morning: "Greater is the power of the Holy Spirit that is in me, than the power coming from the devil that's in the world. That power of God is much stronger than any power that's in the sickness, addiction, anger, worry, fear, stress, and all the other lies coming from the enemy. The resurrection power of the Holy Spirit lives in me, and I'm an overcomer by the blood of the Lamb and by the words of my testimony that come out of my mouth." I quote many scriptures every morning, during the day, and before I go to bed. Why am I doing this? We'll, quoting the scriptures won't necessarily heal me immediately. When I quote the scriptures, I believe that they are relevant and that they are seed for what I need. I'm planting the seed of the Word into my spirit man for my specific need; for healing, for financial needs, for protection and for whatever other need I have. I hear the Word of God. It goes into my spirit man. It creates mustard seed faith in me. Then I speak those faith-filled words again and I believe that I'm going to receive what I've been saying. I water the Word-seed that I have planted in my spirit man by believing and thanking God that it's done, even though I cannot see it yet. The seed of the Word will grow, and it will produce the harvest that I have believed God for, because God is faithful.

Remember that confessing and speaking God's Word is calling for the healing, or calling for the need that is already ours, although it has not yet been manifested. God has already provided the healing and all the other needs that we have by dying on the Cross for it. Every time we speak the Word of God it creates faith, and faith then becomes the substance of the things that we hope for, or that what we're expecting God to do, even if we can't see it. For the interest sake, the word hope in the Greek, means to expect, need, want, to ask. Hope is our goal that we're setting. For example, we're expecting and asking God to heal us. Nevertheless, hope does not heal is, faith heals us. Hope needs faith so that we can achieve our goal and receive our healing or miracle. That's one reason why we have to confess and speak God's Word.

I urge you and encourage you to remove all the hybridizing in your faith life. Let's keep our faith pure and powerful. If we have faith as a mustard seed, Jesus said situations will obey us; nothing will be impossible for us. We have to start speaking to ourselves, just like the woman with the issue of blood did. Start speaking into your own life, into your own situations. Believe that what you are saying and praying for, you will receive. Tell your body to be healed, tell your body to refuse and to resist sickness, to reject sickness, and to only accept the healing power of God. Your body is a living entity and it will listen to your voice and commandments. Say it to yourself until you believe it. Let it become part of you.

Speak to your finances, speak to your marriage, speak to the attacks coming against you and command them to be removed and to be cast into the sea. Speak to the bad weather storms. Jesus did and the storm listened to Him, it'll listen to us too! Whatever you speak too, must obey you because you are speaking God's Word. Speak life and salvation into your loved one's life. Speak and declare that they are saved and healed. Call them into the kingdom of God and call those things that are not as if though they are; call all of them saved and healed. Never ever give up on God and His promises. Remember that we're fighting a spiritual fight. The Word of God which is the sword of the Spirit is a spiritual weapon. Use it by speaking the scriptures against the attacks of the enemy. Walk around swinging that sword around in every direction using it against any attack all day long and keeping the enemy far away from you. I want to leave you with some familiar words that I'm sure you have heard over and over again throughout this book, as they were spoken by Jesus while He was on earth.

"Go; your faith has healed you!" I want to encourage you to go, and let your mustard seed faith make you whole, heal you, save you and your loved ones, deliver you, and let it prosper you in all things. May you receive all that you desire according to all the promises in God's Word. Go forward, not backwards, towards God's promises that He has promised you, His child. Go forward and receive all God's promises, they are yours.

2 Corinthians 1:20 says; "For all *the promises of God in Him are Yes*, and *in Him Amen*, to the glory of God through us." (emphasis mine). Let it be done unto you according to the power of your mustard seed faith. Stand strong according to your mustard seed faith and always walk, live, and function through mustard seed faith. Always remember this!

There is power in mustard seed faith; believe in this power, and use it!

RECEIVING JESUS AS YOUR SAVIOR AND YOUR HEALER

C hoosing to receive Jesus Christ as your Savior and your Healer is the greatest miracle that t can ever happen to you. It will be the most important decision you'll ever make! If this is your first time, or if it is a recommitment, the Word of God promises in Romans 10:9–10 *"that if you confess with your mouth the Lord Jesus and believe in your heart that God has raised Him from the dead, you will be saved. For with the heart one believes unto righteousness, and with the mouth confession is made unto salvation."* Romans 10:13 says, *"For whoever calls on the name of the Lord shall be saved."* God has done all He can do for your salvation and your healing. He sent Jesus, His only Son, to die for all your sins; all you have to do is believe and receive.

Pray this prayer out loud:

> *Father, I confess and repent of all of my sins. Thank You for sending Jesus to die on the cross for all my sins and*

sickness. I confess and believe that He died, He rose from the dead, and He is sitting at Your right hand. Thank You for forgiving and healing me. Come into my heart, Lord Jesus, and be my Lord, my Savior, and my Healer. Change me from the old man, to a new man. Deliver me, Lord, from every curse, bondage, and every addiction in my life. By faith in Your Word, I now receive my salvation, my healing, and my deliverance. I am now a child of God, born again in my spirit, and You are my Father. Thank You for saving, healing, and delivering me, Lord, in the name of Jesus Christ, amen.

Now you are a brand-new person in Christ. Your old life is in the past. It's gone; it's over, forgiven, and forgotten by God. So you have to let go of it, too. Your new life is in Christ Jesus. Get into a good Bible-teaching, faith-believing church, and serve God with your whole heart. Make sure to read the Word and pray continually. Congratulations, you are now a born-again child of God.

RECEIVING THE
HOLY SPIRIT

N ow that you are born-again, God wants to give
you His supernatural power to be able to live this
new life. He wants to baptize you with the Holy Spirit.
*"If you then, being evil, know how to give good gifts
to your children, how much more will your heavenly
Father give the Holy Spirit to those who ask Him"* (Luke
11:13). You need to be baptized with the Holy Spirit.
This power of God will change your life even more. To
be able to receive this baptism of the Holy Spirit, all
you have to do is ask, believe, and receive. Pray now:

> *Father, I thank You for saving me,
> healing me, and delivering me. I recog-
> nize my need to have Your power to live
> my Christian life. I ask You to baptize
> me with the Holy Ghost and with fire
> right now. Fill me with power from on
> high, so I can be a witness for You. Fill
> me with Your Holy Spirit, Lord. I believe
> and receive it right now by faith. Thank
> You, Lord. I'm baptized with the Holy*

*Spirit. I welcome You, Holy Spirit, into
my life, Amen.*

I congratulate you. You are now full of the supernatural power of the Holy Spirit. You will be hearing some syllables from a heavenly language you don't know. Go ahead and speak these words out loud by faith. You will be releasing God's power from within and building yourself up in the spirit as well (see 1 Cor. 14:2, 4, 14).

ABOUT THE AUTHOR

H ansie Steyn is the founder and president of Hansie Steyn Ministries, Inc. Originally from South Africa, this evangelist, singer, and author currently travels all over America with his family, ministering the Word of God in conferences, revival meetings, live preaching, music broadcasts, and church services. The rich heritage and accent from the nation of South Africa permeates this family's ministry of teaching God's Word, singing Holy Spirit–inspired original songs, prophetic utterances, and praying for the sick. Salvations, signs, wonders, deliverances, miracles, and healings are a part of the Steyns' meetings. Hansie, his wife Jeanette, and their daughter Elizabeth are now living in America.

To contact Hansie Steyn, please email or call:
Hansie Steyn Ministries, Inc.
E-mail them at: hsteyn1@aol.com
Visit them on the web at: www.hansiesteyn.org
facebook.com: hansiesteynministries
Call them for prayer or bookings at:
903–681–2794

Other Books:
By Hansie Steyn

THE KING SAUL SPIRIT

*A Demonic Force of Destruction
That Has To Be Stopped*

THE KING SAUL SPIRIT — ISBN
978–1–60791–533–1

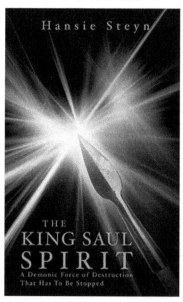

There are many Christians who are rebellious toward God's Word nowadays. They're going out of their way to destroy each other and their churches. I see Christians that hurt, criticize, gossip, and judge each other every day. Churches are splitting up because of infighting—church members disagreeing with and destroying one another. Too many ministers are leaving the pulpit and missing God's call on their lives. Do we have to fight each other? There is no scripture that says we should. Something is wrong when Christians are being used to destroy Christians. Something must be behind this destruction process. So, why are Christians giving in to this attack? This book will help you to identify and understand how to counterattack this evil demonic attack from the *King Saul Spirit*.

HAVE YOU PUT ON
YOUR ARMOR TODAY?

*A Practical Way To Protect Yourself
Against the Enemy*

HAVE YOU PUT ON YOUR ARMOR
TODAY — ISBN
978–1–60791–533–1

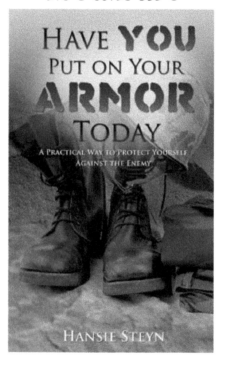

I would like to explain to you how we as Christians should protect our families, our marriages, homes, and churches by putting on the whole armor of God in a practical way. If what I'm going to explain to you can keep you out of a divorce court and stop the anger, strife, and evil in your house and church, will you put on the whole armor of God in a real and practical way? Well, of course! Who wouldn't want to put on the armor of God, right? Well, it's no use having the armor in your house if you don't have a workable plan for putting it on and using it. That's obvious. So let's learn to do it in a practical way that you can perform every day. In this book, I intend to explain the practical application of the armor of God.

CPSIA information can be obtained
at www.ICGtesting.com
Printed in the USA
LVHW032300211218
601146LV00007B/1/P